WELCOME

Locomotive Services Limited Class 47/4 D1944 (47501) *Craftsman* powers past the 103 mile post near Atherstone with the 1Z26 0935 Oxford to Crewe private charter on April 21, 2018, almost 52 years after it entered service. (Graham Nuttall)

Welcome to this special publication dedicated to the Sulzer-powered locomotives that served Britain's railways from the late 1950s. The Swiss engineering company Sulzer had a long history developing diesel engines and was an early exponent of marrying the technology to rail transport. Its work before World War Two stood it in good stead after the conflict ended in 1945 and it was soon supplying diesel engines of varying sizes to railways in Europe and around the world.

With the publishing of British Railways' 1955 Modernisation Plan another huge opportunity opened up and Sulzer found itself providing hundreds of power units for Type 2, 3 and 4 locos well into the 1960s. Its engines were only matched in number by its main rival in the UK market, English Electric. A notable difference between the two was the engine configuration, with EE favouring the V layout while Sulzer preferred an in-line cylinder arrangement. To produce more powerful engines developing more than 2,000hp for Type 4 locos, Sulzer chose to put two in-line six units side by side to create a 12-cylinder unit that drove a single output shaft to turn the generator. This did produce a heavy power unit, and made some components difficult to access for maintenance, but the low-revving four strokes were very reliable, particularly those fitted to the British Railways' Peaks and also in the Class 47, once they were de-rated.

Today the only Sulzer-powered locos still regularly active on the main line are some Class 47s, although a handful of Class 25s and 33s can also be seen on the network, while lenty more, including 26s and 27s, can be found active in preservation. That is quite remarkable given that most are approaching 60 years old and is testament to the engineering and near bulletproof design of the Sulzer diesels.

Mark Nicholls
Editor

CONTENTS

6	Sulzer – Swiss Excellence	**28**	Class 26/27	**70**	*Kestrel*
10	Class 24/25	**42**	Class 33	**78**	Preserved Sulzers
24	*Lion*	**52**	Class 44-46 Peaks	**84**	Class 47

COVER IMAGE: Class 47/4 47567 *Red Star* nears Dainton Summit with the 1427 Paddington to Penzance on July 6, 1985. (John Whiteley)

THIS PAGE: With the impressive York Station as a backdrop, Sulzer-powered Class 45/0 45012 departs to the south with a cross country service on September 1, 1975. *(John Whiteley)*

Editor: Mark Nicholls
Written by: Mark Nicholls, David Clough and Ian McLean
Design: Andy O'Neil, Tracey Croft

Editorial Address
Railways Illustrated, Key Publishing, PO Box 100,
Stamford, Lincolnshire, PE9 1XQ
Tel: 01780 755131
Web: www.railwaysillustrated.com

Advertising Sales Manager: Sam Clark
Email: sam.clark@keypublishing.com
Tel: 01780 755131
Advertising Sales: Alison Sanders

Advertising Production: Cheryl Thornburn
Email: cheryl.thornburn@keypublishing.com
Tel: 01780 755131 **Fax:** 01780 757261

Subscription / Mail Order
Key Publishing Ltd, PO Box 300, Stamford, Lincs, PE9 1NA
Tel: 01780 480404 Fax: 01780 757812
Subscriptions email: subs@keypublishing.com
Mail Order email: orders@keypublishing.com
Website: www.keypublishing.com/shop

PUBLISHING
Group CEO and Publisher: Adrian Cox
Commercial Director: Ann Saundry
Group Marketing Manager: Martin Steele
Webmaster: Simon Russell

Key Publishing Ltd
PO Box 100,
Stamford,
Lincolnshire, PE9 1XP, UK
Website: www.keypublishing.com

Origination and Printing
Precision Colour Printing Ltd, Haldane,
Halesfield 1, Telford, Shropshire. TF7 4QQ

Distribution
Seymour Distribution Ltd, 2 Poultry Avenue, London, EC1A 9PU
Enquiries Line: +44 (0)207 429 4000

We are unable to guarantee the bonafides of any of our advertisers. Readers are strongly recommended to take their own precautions before parting with any information or item of value, including, but not limited to, money, manuscripts, photographs or personal information in response to any advertisements within this publication.

© Key Publishing Ltd 2018
All rights reserved. No part of this magazine may be reproduced or transmitted in any form by any means, electronic or mechanical, including photocopying, recording or by any information storage and retrieval system, without prior permission in writing from the copyright owner. Multiple copying of the contents of the magazine without prior written approval is not permitted.

INTRODUCTION | Sulzer - Swiss Excellence

SULZER
SWISS EXCELLENCE

Switzerland might not really spring to mind as a country that built diesel engines but indigenous company Sulzer did just that, and in huge numbers, exporting all across the world.

For British railway enthusiasts the name Sulzer means one thing – diesel engines. But the Swiss company has, and still does, produce far more products than that. It was formed way back in 1775 by Salomon Sulzer-Bernet and established as Sulzer Brothers Ltd in 1834 in Winterthur, Switzerland. During its early years the firm was involved in the development of shuttleless weaving, with its primary business the production of looms.

Engineer Rudolf Diesel worked for the company in the late 1800s and in 1893 Sulzer acquired some rights to diesel engines, going on to produce its first one in the early 1890s.

Two of the UK's first loco types to use Sulzer diesel engines, the BR Type 2 and Type 4 developed in the late 1950s and early 1960s. Two Type 2s flank a pair of Type 4 Peaks at Holbeck Depot, Leeds, on February 19, 1963. (John Whiteley)

During the 1930s and 1940s Sulzer entered the rail market by developing a series of diesel engines that were used in various locomotives in Africa, Australia, Europe, South America and the UK. However, during World War Two it was blacklisted because it traded with Axis nations.

Coming up to date, the company trades across the world in several disparate industrial sectors, although less so in the diesel engine sector.

Diesel evolution
In 1912 a consortium of Sulzer-Diesel-Klose & Borsig built the first large diesel railway locomotive. It weighed 95 tons, was powered by a valve-less two stroke 4LV38 with a direct drive, rated at 1,000hp, and was known as the 'Thermolokomotive'. In practice it was not successful, due mainly to the direct drive arrangement. In the meantime, Sulzer concentrated on producing smaller engines for use in shunting locos and railcars. Among the latter were five built for Prussia and Saxony Railways and delivered in 1914. They were powered by a 6LV26 four stroke air blast V engine producing 200hp at 440rpm. World War One then intervened, although Sulzer did buy back two of the railcars and modified the engines with the addition of electric starting and direct fuel injection – the first such application for rail use. The two railcars were sold to the Val-de-Travers

6 SULZER POWER

www.railwaysillustrated.co.uk

INTRODUCTION | Sulzer - Swiss Excellence

Probably the firm's greatest breakthrough came in the mid-1930s when the LD range appeared; an engine that was to continue development for decades

Railway in 1923 and one is preserved, believed to be the oldest Sulzer-powered rail vehicle in the world.

The LV type engine was developed right through the 1920s and included an eight cylinder model of 250hp. Swiss Federal Railways used one in a railcar and a Tunisian loco was fitted with another that lasted more than 30 years. However, Sulzer was eager to produce larger designs for the railway market in order to keep pace with other manufacturers. A series of engines rated between 420hp and 1,000hp was produced using a standard format, with different cylinder sizes being the primary difference. Among the features put into wider practice was the use of a steel frame to support both engine and generator assembly, as well as the use of fuel injection.

Between the wars Sulzer became the first diesel engine producer to provide complete locos as a main contractor. Probably the firm's greatest breakthrough came in the mid-1930s when the LD range appeared; an engine that was to continue development for decades and was produced for 50 years and specifically designed for rail application. In its early years the LD was available in the 400hp-2,200hp range and used different cylinder sizes plus a series of features common throughout the range. Among them was the use of large cast steel transversals welded into a mild steel crankcase, which was itself an integral part of the frame supporting the engine and generator. Welded steel plate was used for the cylinder block and the main bearings had fine adjustment wedges incorporated to avoid the need for studded top or bottom caps.

As World War Two commenced, 6LDA25 power units were in use in Algeria, France, Madagascar and Senegal, while a pair of Swiss locos were using 1,200hp 8LDA28s. However, it was the appearance of twin-unit locos for France and Romania that was a particularly significant development. Each featured a double bank 12LDA31 engine producing 2,200hp at 700rpm. The 12LD was simply two six-cylinder engines arranged side by side with gearing

INTRODUCTION | Sulzer - Swiss Excellence

The Sulzer 12LDA28A engine is lowered in to Type 4 D2 in bay 3 of Derby Works' Erecting Shop No 8 on July 31, 1959. (John Tidmarsh)

provided to combine their output to drive a single generator. The engine was the first of its type, but was to be widely used in the UK, Europe and China. Prior to World War Two 87 Sulzer-powered locos, railcars and generator sets had been produced.

Post war boom
With the globe back to relative peace after 1945, orders once again began to flood in. Alstom-built locos were being exported heavily to French colonies and Sulzer engines featured in most of them. Other manufacturers were also exporting heavily and many featured Sulzer power units, notably the 6LDA25 and 8LDA25 models.

Development continued apace during the 1950s, mainly through the use of new materials and construction techniques, all of which helped speed up production rates. This was vital as Sulzer engines were in huge demand from across Europe and further afield. It was the 6LDA28 engine that really got the ball rolling, notably in Ireland where two locos built at the Inchicore workshops in 1950/51 used a 915hp version, later uprated to 960hp. The engine was also ordered by Australia, Sierra Leone and Ireland, again during the mid-1950s. This simply paved the way for massive orders that came after the release of the British Railways 1955 Modernisation Plan. The power unit was chosen to power the British Rail and BRCW Type 2s (Classes 24/25 and 26/27), while the 8LDA28 was selected for the BRCW Type 3 (Class 33). Further orders for the 6LDA25 came from around the world, with the power output increasing to 1,400hp for some.

In an effort to increase the power of the LDA series, Sulzer built two six cylinder prototypes in 1962, rated at 1,700hp at 850rpm and designated as the LDA28-R. Both were built in the UK by Vickers Armstrong, with one being sent to Winterthur to undergo tests and the other being fitted in a BR Type 2. However, the project was cancelled in 1967 and the chosen loco, D5299, was eventually delivered with a standard 6LDA28B.

After the war the double bank 12LDA31 continued to be used in the French and Romanian locos, but it was not developed further. Instead, a slightly smaller variant, the 12LDA28, was selected for further investment, mainly because of its size and lighter weight. A 2,000hp version was exported to France for use in locos around Paris. In the UK a 2,300hp variant was used to power the first BR-designed Type 4 (later Class 44), and was later uprated to 2,500hp for use in the rest of the Peak fleet. The unit was further enhanced to produce 2,750hp in 12LDA28C form and used in the BRCW prototype *Lion* and later the standard BR Type 4 (Class 47). The power

INTRODUCTION | Sulzer - Swiss Excellence

A wheel-less 08911 shunter is jacked up behind the 12LDA28C power unit for 47743 at Crewe Works on August 16, 1996. *(Rail Photoprints/Hugh Ballantyne)*

A partly sectioned Sulzer 6LDA28 straight six diesel engine on display at the National Railway Museum, York. *(Wikipedia Commons/Rept0n1x)*

The first of the major BR designs to be equipped with Sulzer engines was the Type 2, later Class 24/25. Still wearing BR green, but with its TOPS numbers and double arrow symbol applied, 24092 awaits its next duty at Warrington in June 1974. *(Rail Photoprints)*

unit was not developed further, and some issues were encountered with those fitted to Class 47s, leading to the units being de-rated to 2,580hp.

Two V designs, the 1,750hp 8LVA24 and the 650hp 12LVA24, were used in French locos, and were also fitted to the ten Class 47 lookalikes exported to Cuba in 1965. A further five 12LVA24 were used in five Brush Type 4s (Class 48), although these were later fitted with standard 12LDA28C units. The final development of the twin-bank concept was the massive 4,000hp 16LVA24 power unit used in HS4000 *Kestrel*; the engine was the largest and most powerful that Sulzer produced for the rail market.

Meanwhile across the Atlantic in the US, loco rebuilder Morrison-Knudsen fitted several Sulzer engines to a variety of locos. Among the engines used were the 6ASL25/30 and 8ASL25/30 marine power plants, as well as 16 ASV25/30 3,600hp units to AT&SF and Union Pacific locos, although they were not a success.

Recent trading

Sulzer decided to sell off its diesel engine division to a separate company named New Sulzer Diesel (NSD) in 1990. It retained only a small share in the new venture, which was then absorbed by Wärtsilä to create Wärtsilä NSD in 1997. The new firm also produced the world's largest diesel engine – the Wärtsilä-Sulzer RTA96-C – capable of developing 107,390hp; the largest version being 44ft high, 87ft long and weighing more than 2,300 tons. It powers giant container ships.

Meanwhile, Sulzer now has divisions around the world and excels in many other fields, including flow control and applicators, gas and steam turbines, pumps, compressors, motors, generators, production, transport and processing of crude oil and its derivatives, the supply, treatment and transport of water as well as wastewater collection, fossil-fired, nuclear and renewable power generation, pulp and paper, fertilisers, mixing and dispensing systems for the adhesives and dental markets, precise application systems for liquid colour cosmetics and beauty accessories, polymerisation technology for the production of PLA (polylactic acid) and EPS (expandable polystyrene), carbon capture and storage, wastewater treatment and desalination, and much more. The company has come a long way since 1834.

But for the readers of this publication, Sulzer's contribution to the UK rail scene will be of most interest. Its only real rival, in terms of numbers, was English Electric, and between them they helped to power some of the most iconic diesel locomotives to grace Britain's railways. **S**

FEATURE | BR/Sulzer Type 2 (Class 24 and 25)

JACK
OF ALL TRADES
Classes 24 and 25

The power range between Type 1 and 4 was only 1,000hp but, of the two in between, the British Railways/Sulzer Type 2 was built in the largest numbers, eventually totalling 478 examples.

The most numerous locomotive built to fulfil the Type 2 power category was designed by British Railways and powered by either the Sulzer 6LDA 28A or B diesel engine. It was a common sight right across the UK rail network, apart from the Southern Region, although even there early examples were deployed in the late 1950s. It was the Midland and Scottish Regions in particular that were home to the majority of the fleet, with others going to the Eastern and Western Regions.

Concept

British Railway's Derby Locomotive Works designed the standard D11 and D12 classification (later Type 2) to meet a British Transport Commission requirement to replace lower powered steam locos. The resultant Bo-Bo was first introduced in 1958, with the initial order of 20 examples built at Derby, which was selected because of its experience with previous diesels, such as shunting locos that it had been building since 1939, the

BR/Sulzer Type 2 (Class 24 and 25) | **FEATURE**

A pair of Class 25/3s, 25209 and 25296, head past New Mills South Junction with a heavy rake of Presflo cement wagons on August 13, 1983. (Gavin Morrsion)

FEATURE | BR/Sulzer Type 2 (Class 24 and 25)

LMS Twins and the Fell 2,000hp diesel-mechanical No 10100.

Initial experience with the new loco was positive and it was not long before more orders were placed. These went to Derby, Crewe and Darlington, as well as some to Beyer Peacock at Gorton in Manchester. Although this was meant to speed up deliveries, the final examples of the 478 built didn't emerge until 1967. The first batches were of what was to become the 1,160hp Class 24 (D5000-5150); these were followed by the slightly more powerful Class 25 (D5151-5299 and D7500-7677).

Design and equipment

In keeping with many other early diesel designs, the loco body was fairly simple; the aim being to permit easy and rapid mass production. Full width cabs were initially equipped with gangway doors allowing connection to a second locomotive, particularly if the steam heating boiler was in use on that second loco. The doors were fitted to the first 233 locos, but after that they were discontinued and the cab front redesigned with a larger centre window to match the depth of the other two. As the need for the connecting doors reduced, and because they were draughty, they were gradually removed and a metal panel was welded over the hole.

The body structure was of a trussed girder design to help save weight, while a bridge-girder framework supported the engine and generator. Two primary longitudinal members formed the underframe and cleverly they included two channel sections with plates top and bottom that provided ducting for air to cool the traction motors. The bodysides were of open-girder frame construction that attached to the underframe, with several grills to allow air into the engine

The scene inside the Derby Works erecting shop on June 17, 1959, with Type 2s D5020, 5021 and 5023 on the right and Type 4s (Class 44) D3, 4 and 5 on the left.
(John Tidmarsh)

> In keeping with many other early diesel designs, the loco body was fairly simple; the aim being to permit easy and rapid mass production.

BR/Sulzer Type 2 D5128 leads BRCW Type 2 D5331 at Hilton Junction after leaving Perth with a train for Edinburgh on April 20, 1965.
(John Whiteley)

From left to right, newly completed D5008, D5007 and D5006 stand outside 8 Shop (erecting shop) on January 27, 1959. (John Tidmarsh)

room for the engine and radiators. In practice this wasn't the ideal solution as the grills, through which air was filtered, still allowed in dust and debris from outside, which caused reliability issues. Later versions of the Class 25 had all the grills moved to the cantrail level and that greatly reduced the problem. Staying with the roof, it was completely removable between the two cabs, providing quick and easy access to the major components to allow easy removal during maintenance and overhaul. Aluminium doors were provided above the diesel engine too.

The original locos, later to become Class 24, had a fibreglass cab roof and used the disc type of train description mounted on the cab front. After the 114th loco was finished, subsequent examples and all of the Class 25s employed a roof-mounted four-digit headcode box.

Internally the Type 2s resembled many other designs by having three compartments – one for the Stone-Vapor steam heating boiler (No 2 end), the larger centre section for the engine, generator and control cubicle, plus auxiliary equipment such as a compressor and exhauster and traction motor blowers and, finally, a compartment for the radiators and ●

Almost complete but yet to be painted, the body of Type 2 D5008 is lowered onto its bogies at BR Derby Works in late 1958. (Colin Marsden Collection)

A snow-covered Pen-y-Ghent forms the background as Type 2 D5097 makes slow progress on the climb to Blea Moor at Horton in Ribblesdale on the Settle to Carlisle line with a coal train on November 29, 1969. (Gavin Morrison)

FEATURE | BR/Sulzer Type 2 (Class 24 and 25)

Towards the end of its career, 24124 takes a breather between duties at Haymarket Depot on April 20, 1976. It was withdrawn in December that year and disposed of at Swindon Works in May 1977. (Gavin Morrison)

Type 2 D5178 passes Shipley with the 1514 Leeds City to Morecambe and Carnforth service on April 29, 1963. The loco entered traffic at Holbeck (55A) in February 1963 and lasted until December 1980 when it was withdrawn at Haymarket as 25028. (John Whiteley)

BR/Sulzer Type 2 (Class 24) Technical data		
Class:	24/0	24/1
Builders:	BR Derby, Crewe	BR Crewe, Derby and Darlington
Introduced:	1958-59	1959-1961
Number series:	D5000-D5049	D5050-D5150
TOPS number series:	24001-24049	24050-24150
Former class codes:	D11/1, later 11/1	D11/3, later 11/1A
Wheel arrangement:	Bo-Bo	Bo-Bo
Route availability:	6	6
Multiple working:	Blue Star	Blue Star
Engine:	Sulzer 6LDA28A	Sulzer 6LDA28A
Horsepower:	1,160hp (865kW)	1,160hp (865kW)
Main generator type:	BTH RTB15656	BTH RTB15656
Aux generator type:	BTH RTB7440	BTH RTB7440
Traction motor type:	BTH 137 BY	BTH 137 BY
Brakes (Loco):	Air	Air
Brakes (Train):	Vacuum	Vacuum
Brake force:	38 tonnes	38 tonnes
Maximum Tractive effort:	40,000lb (178kN)	40,000lb (178kN)
Power at rail:	843hp (629kW)	843hp (629kW)
Length:	50ft 6in (15.39m)	50ft 6in (15/39m)
Width:	8ft 10in (2.70m)	8ft 10in (2.70m)
Height:	12ft 8in (3.86m)	12ft 8in (3.86m)
Weight:	77-79 tonnes	71-73 tonnes
Wheel diameter:	3ft 9in (1.14m)	3ft 9in (1.14m)
Max speed:	75mph (121km/h)	75mph (121km/h)
Steam Heating:	Stones OK 4616	Stones OK 4616 or 4610
Fuel tank capacity:	630gal (2,384lit)	630gal (2,384lit)
Cooling water capacity:	187gal (708lit)	187gal (708lit)
Lub oil capacity:	100gal (378lit)	100gal (378lit)
Boiler water capacity:	600gal (2,271lit)	600gal (2,271lit)

fan assembly. However, a considerable number were built without a train heating boiler, with a compensating concrete ballast weight installed instead.

The pressure-charged Sulzer 6LDA28 A provided 1,160hp and was fitted to the first 150 locos (Class 24), with the more powerful charge-air cooled 1,250hp 6LDA28 B used to power the remaining fleet (Class 25). Self-draining radiators were used to help avoid frost damage, while the cooling fan was electrically powered and controlled by a thermostat.

The first 50 Types 2s (D5000-49) were fitted with British Thomson-Houston generators, with the output controlled by a load regulator that was governed by a rheostat in the exciter field. The rest of the build was not fitted with an exciter and instead used separate shunt and differential windings with load control in the separate fields. There was also a slight variation for locos D5151-75 (Class 25/0s) in that the main generator was rated at 750/545V, 1090/1500A instead of 780/545V, 1050/1500A. On all locos the auxiliary generator was mounted above and driven by a belt.

Simple box-frame Bo-Bo bogies were used, of a riveted and welded construction. They were of outside frame design and used a spring-plank bolster arrangement and four spring links. Coil springs were utilised for bolster and axleboxes, with the latter fitted with equalising beam and hydraulic shock absorbers. To determine the best equipment for the first 20 locos, ten were fitted with Athermos plain-bearing, pressure-lubricated axleboxes, while the other ten had SKF roller bearing boxes.

The brake system was by Davies & Metcalfe and was of the Oerlikon type with Westinghouse and Davies & Metcalfe brake cylinders. To start with it comprised a vacuum train brake and air brakes on the loco, but as air-braked trains became more numerous, dual air/vacuum train brakes were installed.

To permit running in multiple, Blue Star electro-pneumatic equipment was

Awaiting the chop, Class 24 24066 stands in yard at Doncaster Works on June 18, 1978. The loco was withdrawn at Haymarket in February 1976 and was finally broken up in August 1978. (Gavin Morrison)

A BR/Sulzer Type 2, thought to be D5130, heads a short passenger service along the former Great North of Scotland Railway route between Cullen and Portsoy. The photos is believed to be at either Tochieneal or Glassaugh and the date sometime in the early 1960s. The station had long since closed, and the line followed suit in 1968. (Fergus Johnson/John Whiteley collection)

16 SULZER POWER www.railwaysillustrated.co.uk

BR/Sulzer Type 2 (Class 24 and 25) | FEATURE

The second of the 1,250hp Type 2s, D5152 (later Class 25/0 25002), fresh off the production line at Darlington Works on April 22, 1961. It entered service the following month and remained in traffic until December 1980 when it was retired from Eastfield. (Mike Goodfield)

Former departmental Class 24 ADB968009 (24142) dumped out of use at Healey Mills on April 24, 1983. Its departmental role as a static train heating unit lasted from August 1976 until September 1982, and it was finally scrapped by Coopers Metals in Sheffield in May 1984. (Gavin Morrison)

provided, allowing two locos to be driven from one cab, including any class of loco with the same system.

The four traction motors were of the axle-hung traction nose-suspended type with rubber mountings. Different traction motors were used during the Type 2's production with locos D5000-D5175 fitted with the BTH 137BY and 137BX type, providing 222hp (BY) or 245hp (BX). All motors were permanently connected in parallel. Interestingly, different gear ratios were employed, with D5000-D5150 using one of 16:81 and having a maximum speed of 75mph, while D5151-75 (Class 25/0) used a ratio of 18:79 and had a top speed of 90mph. All the remaining locos that became Class 25s used Associated Electrical Industries 253AY traction motors rated at 234hp.

> **The engine was assembled and tested at the Winterthur factory in Switzerland and used a four-valve cylinder head in a strengthened case.**

The locos' batteries, fuel tank and water tank (for the steam heating boiler, if fitted) were slung beneath the body between the bogies. The batteries could be pulled out on rails for access, maintenance and changing.

An interesting anecdote concerns D5299, in which it was planned to fit a modified Sulzer 6LDA28-R engine developing 1750hp. The engine was assembled and tested at the Winterthur factory in Switzerland and used a four-valve cylinder head in a strengthened case. The prototype was built, but the project was abandoned in 1965 and the loco entered service in standard form, albeit a whole year after it was structurally complete.

Roll out and initial use

Work on the first of the Type 2s, D5000, commenced at Derby in the autumn of 1957. It first appeared in public at Marylebone station on July 25, 1958 when it was officially 'rolled out' to the Chairman of the BTC, Sir Brian Robertson, railway staff and the press. The first batch of 20 went to the London Midland Region, with early trials using D5000 held between Derby and Millers Dale, as well as on the Derby-Manchester-Liverpool route. The fleet was allocated to Crewe, but on loan to Derby.

Meanwhile, a plan was drawn up to send 15 of them to the Southern Region while it awaited delivery of its own BRCW Type 3s; by early 1959 they started to arrive at the South Eastern Division, based at Hither Green, with major maintenance undertaken at Eastleigh Works. Unfortunately, the Southerns Region's Civil Engineer was not happy with the locos' weight, which exceeded the route weight limit by five tons. To solve the problem the steam heating boiler and various fittings were removed temporarily, but even then some route availability restrictions remained.

The locos were widely used on Southern metals, hauling a variety of traffic, but in winter were mostly limited to freight

Sulzer Type (Class 25) Technical data				
Class:	25/0	25/1	25/2	25/3
Builders:	BR Darlington	BR Darlington	BR Darlington	BR Derby
		BR Derby	BR Derby	Beyer Peacock
Introduced:	1961-62	1963	1963-66	1965-67
Number series:	D5151-D5175	D5176-D5232	D5233-D7597	D7598-D7677
TOPS number series:	25001-25025	25026-25082	25083-25247	25248-25327
Former class codes:	D12/1, later 12/1	D12/1, later 12/1	D12/1, later 12/1	D12/1, later 12/1
Wheel arrangement:	Bo-Bo	Bo-Bo	Bo-Bo	Bo-Bo
Route availability:	5	5	5	5
Multiple working:	Blue Star	Blue Star	Blue Star	Blue Star
Engine:	Sulzer 6LDA28B	Sulzer 6LDA28B	Sulzer 6LDA28B	Sulzer 6LDA28B
Horsepower:	1,250hp (932kW)	1,250hp (932kW)	1,250hp (932kW)	1,250hp (932kW)
Main generator type:	AEI RTB 15656	AEI RTB 15656	AEI RTB 15656	AEI RTB 15656
Aux generator type:	AEI RTB 7440	AEI RTB 7440	AEI RTB 7440	AEI RTB 7440
Traction motor type:	AEI 137BX	AEI 253AY	AEI 253AY	AEI 253AY
Brakes (Loco):	Air	Air	Air	Air
Brakes (Train):	Vacuum	Vacuum/Dual	Vacuum/Dual	Vacuum/Dual
Brake force:	38 tonnes	38 tonnes	38 tonnes	38 tonnes
Maximum Tractive effort:	45,000lb (200kN)	45,000lb (200kN)	45,000lb (200kN)	45,000lb (200kN)
Power at rail:	949hp (708kW)	949hp (708kW)	949hp (708kW)	949hp (708kW)
Length:	50ft 6in (15.39m)	50ft 6in (15.39m)	50ft 6in (15.39m)	50ft 6in (15.39m)
Width:	9ft 1in (2.76m)	9ft 1in (2.76m)	9ft 1in (2.76m)	9ft 1in (2.76m)
Height:	12ft 8in (3.86m)	12ft 8in (3.86m)	12ft 8in (3.86m)	12ft 8in (3.86m)
Weight:	72 tonnes	72 tonnes	76 tonnes	76 tonnes
Wheel diameter:	3ft 9in (1.14m)	3ft 9in (1.14m)	3ft 9in (1.14m)	3ft 9in (1.14m)
Max speed:	90 mph (145km/h)	90 mph (145km/h)	90 mph (145km/h)	90 mph (145km/h)
Steam Heating:	Stone 4610	Stone 4610	Stone 4610	Not fitted
Fuel tank capacity:	500gal (1,892lit)	500gal (1,892lit)	500gal (1,892lit)	500gal (1,892lit)
Lub oil capacity:	100gal (378lit)	100gal (378lit)	100gal (378lit)	100gal (378lit)
Boiler water capacity:	580gal (2,195lit)	580gal (2,195lit)	580gal (2,195lit)	Not fitted

FEATURE | BR/Sulzer Type 2 (Class 24 and 25)

With barely a year left for steam on BR, Fairburn 2-6-4T 42145 is piloted though St Dunstans Cutting, Bradford, by Type 2 D5180 with a service for King's Cross on June 16, 1967. The working was a regular one used to train crews on the new diesels. (Gavin Morrison)

BR/Sulzer Type 2 (Class 24 and 25) | **FEATURE**

due to their lack of train heating. The Southern began receiving its Type 3s in 1960, but they only had electric train heating and with most hauled stock equipped only for steam heat, the Type 2s were retained for a while and their boilers reinstated. This required the Civil Engineer to temporarily relax the previous weight restrictions. It was not until 1962 that the Type 2s returned to the London Midland Region.

The additional Type 2 orders meant Derby and Crewe Works began mass production during 1959/60, with the Eastern and North Eastern Regions the first to benefit. Locos were delivered to March, Ipswich and Stratford on the Great Eastern lines, with D5020-29/66-75 from Derby and D5030-65/76-93 coming from Crewe. Shortly afterwards Darlington was added to the builder's list, with its first two locos, D5094/95, going to the Eastern Region and D5096-D5113 to the North Eastern Region at Gateshead, although they were out-based at South Gosforth DMU Depot. Meanwhile in November 1960, D5094 was moved to Finsbury Park for use on cross-London freight trials from Ferme Park to Hither Green and Feltham.

A modification to a small batch of the Type 2s was made in early 1961 at Stratford Works with the addition of 'trip-cocks' to allow them to run on the London Transport widened lines to Moorgate.

Further locos were sent to the NER, including the final 1,160hp Type 2s D5147-50 and the first 1,250hp

> **A modification to a small batch of the Type 2s was made in early 1961 at Stratford Works with the addition of 'trip-cocks' to allow them to run on the London Transport widened lines to Moorgate.**

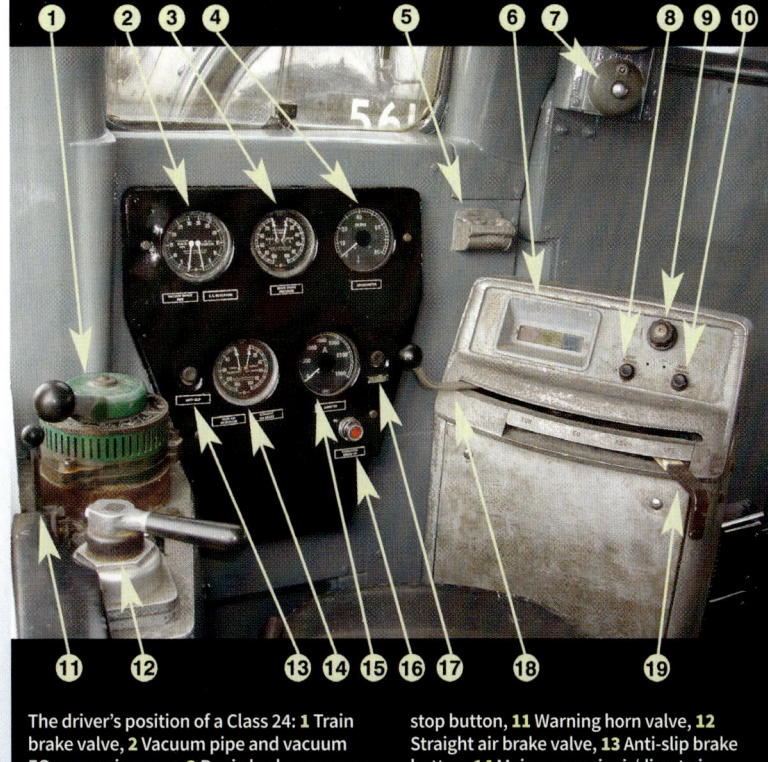

The driver's position of a Class 24: **1** Train brake valve, **2** Vacuum pipe and vacuum EQ reservoir gauge, **3** Bogie brake pressure gauge, **4** Speedometer, **5** Ashtray, **6** Warning lights, red engine stopped, amber wheel slip light, blue general fault light, **7** AWS reset button, **8** Engine start button, **9** Instrument light dimmer switch, **10** Engine stop button, **11** Warning horn valve, **12** Straight air brake valve, **13** Anti-slip brake button, **14** Main reservoir air/direct air brake pressure gauge, **15** Ammeter, **16** Exhauster speed-up button, **17** Brake release button, **18** Power controller, **19** Master switch (off/reverse/engine only/forward). (Paul Fuller)

BOTTOM: Wearing one of the early representations of BR blue on the Class 25/3, D7673 (25323) approaches Ribblehead with a down freight on February 14, 1970. (Gavin Morrison)

BELOW: Two of the 1,250hp Type 2s display the different body styles at Leeds Holbeck Depot on May 10, 1964. D5209 (Class 25/1 25059) is of the original design, with plenty of bodyside grills and cab-to-cab gangways doors, while D5233 was the first of what became the Class 25/2 and has the later styling with all the grills moved above cantrail level and also the revised can end layout. The 25/1 is now preserved at the Keighley & Worth Valley Railway. (Gavin Morrison)

SULZER POWER 19

FEATURE | BR/Sulzer Type 2 (Class 24 and 25)

A particularly grimy Type 2, D7571 (later Class 25/2 25221), passes Bradley Junction to the east of Huddersfield with the SO only Bradford portion of a Poole service on June 21, 1969. The coaches joined a portion from Leeds at Huddersfield before proceeding to the South Coast.
(Gavin Morrison)

versions, D5151-82; they were allocated to Leeds Holbeck, Gateshead and Thornaby. Subsequent transfers saw York receive a few in 1963. The NER began using its Type 2s on the Tyne Dock-Consett iron-ore trains, usually working in pairs to replace the BR Class 9F 2-10-0s. The wagons used on these trains were fitted with air-operated doors, so the locos had an additional air compressor.

The next recipient was Tinsley Depot in Sheffield in 1965 and it took delivery of part of the D7624-49 batch built by Beyer Peacock. The company received an order for 54 locos in 1964, D7624-77, as an attempt to keep its Gorton Foundry facility open. Unfortunately, the firm's finances deteriorated and it asked to be released from the contract, meaning D7660-77 were constructed by BR at Derby.

The London Midland Region finally started to receive more new Type 2s from the autumn of 1960, eventually including D5133-D5146, D5183-D5299, D7500-D7577, D7650-D7659 and D7670-D7697. Furthermore, some inter-regional transfers brought more locos to the LMR. Some were sub-based at Rugby for use on inter-regional services in the Midlands, such as Birmingham to Norwich and Rugby to Euston. At the southern end of the West Coast Main Line Willesden received an allocation for use on outer suburban duties. Multiple working on the Luton to Bonnybridge car trains and use on the Condor freightliner service between

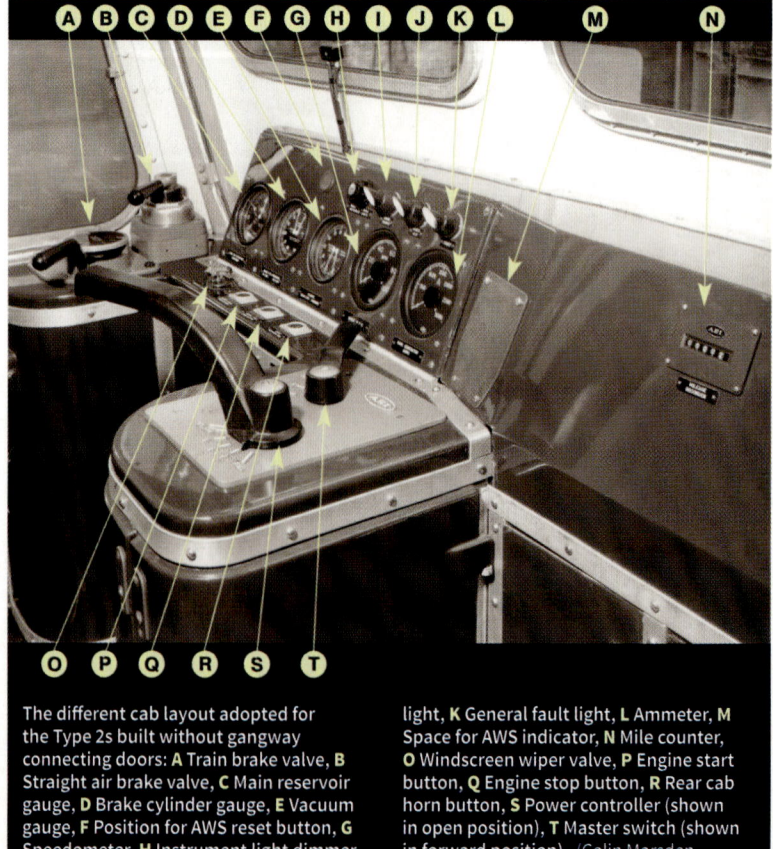

The different cab layout adopted for the Type 2s built without gangway connecting doors: **A** Train brake valve, **B** Straight air brake valve, **C** Main reservoir gauge, **D** Brake cylinder gauge, **E** Vacuum gauge, **F** Position for AWS reset button, **G** Speedometer, **H** Instrument light dimmer switch, **I** Engine stopped light, **J** Wheel slip light, **K** General fault light, **L** Ammeter, **M** Space for AWS indicator, **N** Mile counter, **O** Windscreen wiper valve, **P** Engine start button, **Q** Engine stop button, **R** Rear cab horn button, **S** Power controller (shown in open position), **T** Master switch (shown in forward position). (Colin Marsden Collection)

BR/Sulzer Type 2 (Class 24 and 25) | FEATURE

Hendon in North London and Glasgow began in the early 1960s, although the Condor service was more famous for using Metropolitan Vickers Co-Bos.

Scotland is well known for its use of the Type 2s, but in fact it only received two batches of brand new locos, D5114-32 to Inverness in 1960 and D7611-23 to Eastfield in 1966. The Inverness locos were fitted with twin spot lamps mounted on the gangway doors for use on the Highland line. Progressively more locos arrived in Scotland, partly to replace the less than successful North British Class 21/29s.

The last region to receive the type was the Western, with some Class 25s arriving in 1971 to replace the diesel hydraulic North British Class 22s. The 25s went to Newport, Bristol Bath Road and Laira depots and were used primarily on freight and parcels duties, although by the late 1970s they were also rostered on Cardiff to Crewe and local West of England passenger services.

ETHEL

Electric Train Heating Ex-Locomotive (ETHEL) was popular in the 1970s as a means of providing an electric supply to stabled coaches, particularly

> Electric Train Heating Ex-Locomotive (ETHEL) was popular in the 1970s as a means of providing an electric supply to stabled coaches, particularly air-conditioned examples during the summer.

ETHELs 97251 and 97252 at Glasgow's Eastfield Depot in June 1985. (Stuart Kirkby)

A Sulzer 6LDA28B engine is railed out of the body of a Class 25 at Crewe Works. (Colour Rail)

BELOW: Crewe was always a good place to see both Classes of Type 2s, especially during the 1970s when a host of Class 24s were based at the diesel depot. A decade later and towards the end of their careers 25212, 25297 and 25298 stand alongside Class 45/0 45063 on May 28, 1985. (John Whiteley)

Departmental No	ETHEL No	TOPS No	Introduced	Withdrawn	Notes
97250	ETHEL 1	25310	May-1983	Oct-1987	ADB968024 not worn
97251	ETHEL 2	25305	Aug-1983	Nov-1993	ADB968025 not worn
97252	ETHEL 3	25314	Jul-1983	Nov-1993	ADB968026 not worn

FEATURE | BR/Sulzer Type 2 (Class 24 and 25)

Celebrity Class 25 25322 *Tamworth Castle* was repainted into BR green and numbered D7672 during its final months and was often turned out for railtours. It approaches Saddleworth with the Pathfinder Tours 'Sulzer Salute Railtour', which originated at Swindon using a Class 47, on February 16, 1991. (John Whiteley)

air-conditioned examples during the summer as it kept the interiors cool. Examples of Classes 15 and 24 were initially used, and a second wave of conversions was authorised in 1983 but with a need to be mobile. The modified locos would be formed up between the train engine and the coaches, meaning a non-ETH fitted loco could haul the train. The concept was employed in Scotland, where ETH-fitted stock was being used but ETH locos were in short supply, especially on routes with restrictive route availability.

The three locos chosen for the project were converted at Aberdeen Ferryhill depot (see table on previous page.) The locos wore the 'names' ETHEL 1 to ETHEL 3 and remained in service for around three years on Scottish services until ETH-fitted locos made them redundant. Afterwards they still found use on charter trains, including some steam railtours, and were also put to use at various depots and workshops to provide a shore supply.

During its latter years 25322 became an enthusiasts' favourite and was named *Tamworth Castle* and adorned with a modified blue livery. In multiple with 25315, it waits for a fresh crew at Healey Mills with a tank train for Stanlow on March 26, 1989.
(Gavin Morrison)

Class 25/2 25224 leaves Shrewsbury with a Crewe to Cardiff service on February 14, 1981. The Type 2s eventually gave way to Class 33s on the route.
(John Whiteley)

Difficulties

Although the 6LDA28 engines were more sturdy and reliable than the twin-bank 12LDA28 used in the Types 4s, they still had a few problems, notably with welds in the engine structure, but these were easily fixed at BR workshops. There were also issues with leaking cylinder liners, failed transition rubbers, leaking cylinder-head core plugs and fuel starvation, resulting in loss of power. The latter was caused by blocked filter elements. There were also instances of fractured turbocharger water jackets. The rest of the loco caused little concern, but vibration did affect the aluminium parts of the bodywork.

As with other designs, such as the Brush Type 2, the centre gangway meant the driver and secondman positions on each side of it were rather cramped. However, when they were eliminated in the later examples the cab was opened up and the

A dozen Class 25s wait for a tow from Swindon Works to Leicester for scrapping on May 15, 1987. (Gavin Morrison)

BR/Sulzer Type 2 (Class 24 and 25) | FEATURE

Class 24/25 survivors

Number	Location	Status
D5032 (24032)	North Yorkshire Moors Railway	Overhaul
D5054 (24054)	East Lancashire Railway	Overhaul
D5061 (24061)	North Yorkshire Moors Railway	Awaiting overhaul
24081	Gloucestershire Warwickshire Railway	Operational
D5185 (25035)	Great Central Railway	Operational
25057	North Norfolk Railway	Overhaul
25059	Keighley & Worth Valley Railway	Operational
25067	Burton upon Trent	Stored unserviceable
25072	Caledonian Railway	Stored unserviceable
25083	Caledonian Railway	Stored unserviceable
D7523 (25173)	Battlefield Line	Overhaul
D7535 (25185)	Dartmouth Steam Railway	Operational
D7541 (25191)	South Devon Railway	Overhaul
25235	Bo'ness & Kinneil Railway	Overhaul
25244	Kent & East Sussex Railway	Stored unserviceable
D7612 (25262)	South Devon Railway	Operational
25265	Burton upon Trent	Overhaul
D7628 (25278)	North Yorkshire Moors Railway	Operational
25279 (D7629)	Great Central Railway – Nottingham	Operational
D7633 (25283)	Dean Forest Railway	Overhaul
25309	Peak Rail	Stored unserviceable
25313	Weardale Railway	Stored unserviceable
25321	Midland Railway Centre	Operational
25322	Churnet Valley Railway	Overhaul

Two Class 25s, 25215 and 25123, pass Garsdale with a Carlisle to Tinsley mixed freight on November 4, 1981. (John Whiteley)

addition of the deeper centre window helped make for a better environment.

Poor joints between body panels and also the roof often led to water ingress, while a similar problem around the cab caused considerable drafts, which were usually overcome using plenty of masking tape!

When it became necessary to fit the locos with air-braking equipment to provide a dual-brake capability, the lack of internal space made finding a place for a second air compressor difficult. Eventually it was installed on the A side, but it severely restricted access to that part of the loco. The large bodyside grill was found to be an issue in the severe winter of 1962/63 as it let in

During the 1980s great piles of Type 2s at Vic Berry's Leicester scrapyard became quite a talking point. In this view taken on July 26, 1987 25134, 25161 and 25180 wait their turn with the breaker's torch. (John Stretton)

> Towards the end of their careers, Class 25s suffered from a shortage of spare components as well as increasing levels of corrosion.

too much cold air, causing the cooling and steam heating systems to freeze. A solution was to provide removable blanking plates.

Towards the end of their careers, Class 25s suffered from a shortage of spare components as well as increasing levels of corrosion. The first Class 24s started to go in 1969 when deemed uneconomical to repair, with the fleet's major run down coming from 1975. The Class 25s soldiered on for another decade, with the last withdrawn in 1987. Commonly referred to as 'Rats', the 25s became popular for railtours in their final months, and fortunately several have survived into preservation. **S**

FEATURE | D0260 LION

D0260 LION

David Clough examines the brief but chequered history of D0260 Lion, Birmingham Railway Carriage & Wagon Company's ill-fated prototype.

24 SULZER POWER

www.railwaysillustrated.co.uk

D0260 LION | FEATURE

The immaculate loco, fresh from the factory, passes Shrewsbury during one of its initial trials in April 1962. (Rail Photoprints/Hugh Ballantyne collection)

In January 1960, the British Transport Commission published a specification for its future Type 4 requirements. The design was to have an installed horsepower of 2,750, be mounted on six powered axles and have a maximum axle-load of 19tons. Three manufacturers built prototypes against the specification, one of which was Birmingham Railway Carriage & Wagon Co.

Concept

Sulzer was already collaborating with BRCW by supplying the engines for Type 2 and 3 designs under construction for the BTC and this was extended to the engine for the new prototype. A new partner, Associated Electrical Industries, was chosen for the electrical equipment. Sulzer's turbocharged LDA28 engine was installed in a range of configurations for other BR designs, but for the prototype it was developed into the 'C' version by enhancing intercooling and increasing maximum engine speed to 800rpm. These changes meant that the 12LDA28C now produced 2,750bhp and its use in the BRCW prototype made the loco the most powerful single-engine unit in the world. Unlike many other designs that opted for 'V' cylinder arrangements, Sulzer adopted 12 cylinders using two parallel blocks of six.

AEI main, auxiliary and electric train heat generators were fitted, while the company's AEI253 traction motor was already being used for the latest variant of the Derby-built BR/Sulzer Type 2. Motor gearing for the new Type 4 was for 100mph.

Designing the mechanical parts was a substantial task because of the need to produce a Co Co wheel arrangement with a 19-ton maximum axle-load. Weight was saved in all aspects of the body's construction and the relatively new practice of employing a load-bearing, stressed body skin kept down weight. Fluting of the mild steel plates below waist level was a novel touch to enhance appearance and probably also increased strength, while extensive use was made of asbestos for bodyside insulation. An unusual feature was a pneumatically operated main fibreglass roof section, which could be ➔

FEATURE | D0260 LION

raised to give easy access to the top of the Sulzer engine during maintenance. Adjacent to this were oil-wetted filters to supply clean air to the engine compartment, while the radiators were mounted at roof level. The French-supplied mild steel bogies were the UK's first to use the Alstom system of twin rubber cone body supports and radius arm-guided axle boxes. The driver's power handle was marked 'Off', 'Full' and 'Top'. The last position cut off train heating to give extra power for traction, allowing the engine rpm to increase to its maximum. Unusually, the driver's instruments used ultra-violet illumination. Ammeters recorded motor current, rather than the usual British practice of main generator current.

External styling was handled by Wilkes & Ashmore, which had already worked on the Beyer Peacock Type 3 Hymek and would also style the new Brush Type 4. The loco was finished in a striking, if utterly impractical, white livery. At 114tons in working order, it was within the stipulated 19-ton axle-load limit. Construction at the BRCW works at Smethwick, West Midlands was complete by April 1962 and works number DEL260 assigned. This number was expanded into D0260 to serve as the BR stock number, while the name *Lion* was also applied. It was exhibited at Marylebone Station on May 6, a regular practice for new loco designs because of the close proximity to the BTC headquarters.

Trials

A sensible allocation to the Western Region's Wolverhampton Stafford Road shed meant the BRCW works was nearby and the prototype became the first main line diesel to be deployed in the district. Crew training runs commenced between Birmingham and Shrewsbury, using two Wolverhampton Stafford Road tutor drivers. On May 15, 1962, D0260 was introduced on revenue-earning services between Wolverhampton and Paddington, working up with the 0735 and back with the 1810, with a midday fill-in turn to Birmingham. Performance and riding qualities were reported to be excellent and

Lion under construction at BRCW's Smethwick facility on June 23, 1961. At the time the superstructure was undergoing strain gauge tests. To simulate weight of the power unit, generator and train heating boiler heavy blocks were inserted in the relevant positions. (Colin J Marsden collection)

26 SULZER POWER   www.railwaysillustrated.co.uk

D0260 LION | FEATURE

LEFT: *Lion* passes through High Wycombe with a test train on February 2, 1962. (Colour-Rail/C Leigh-jones)

RIGHT, TOP: D0260 *Lion* passes Warwick with a WR express on May 16, 1962. (Colour-Rail)

RIGHT: The impressive white prototype stands outside the BRCW Smethwick Works on Good Friday, April 20, 1962. The board in front reads 'Prototype Type 4 2,750hp diesel electric locomotive – Co-Co wheel arrangement, designed and built by the Birmingham Rly Carriage & Wagon Co Ltd & fitted with Sulzer 12LDA28C diesel engine and Associated Electrical Industries traction & control equipment'. (Rail-Online)

BELOW: D0260 *Lion* awaits its next turn of duty at Ranelagh Bridge stabling point at Royal Oak, Paddington, during 1962. It shares the once busy facility with Warship D818 *Glory* and Hymek D7069. (Colin J Marsden collection)

Technical data	
Number	D0260
Introduced	1962
Withdrawn	1964
Wheel Arrangement	Co Co
Engine	Sulzer 12LDA28C
Cylinders	12 (two banks of six)
Horsepower	2,750
Main Generator	AEI TG5303
Traction Motors	AEI253
Train Heat (electric)	AEI AG106
Train Heat (steam)	Spanner IIIB
Brakes (loco)	Air
Brakes (train)	Vacuum
Maximum Tractive Effort	55,000lb
Continuous Tractive Effort	30,000lb
Length	63ft 6in
Width	8ft 10in
Height	12ft 9 ¾in
Weight	114 tons
Wheel diameter	3ft 9in
Max speed	100mph
Fuel Tank	850 gallons
Number Built	1

train running data shows speeds of up to 105mph were attained.

It was then put through a series of dynamometer car trials between July 24 and August 15. These included restarting a 569-ton train on the steepest sections of the South Devon banks, followed by restarting a 19-coach 635-ton load up the Lickey Incline. During the latter the main generator was described as sparking like a Catherine wheel, which was due to a technical fault that was rectified.

Lion was returned to BRCW to resolve the issues that had emerged during the trials, not reappearing until March 1963. On September 9 it was transferred to the Eastern Region and based at Finsbury Park, from where it worked the Yorkshire Pullman between King's Cross and Leeds and the Master Cutler to Sheffield. However, on November 12 a large electrical fault caused a minor explosion in the control cubicle. Engineers from AEI had to rebuild the cubicle and re-test the loco before returning it to Eastern Region use by the year-end. It was redeployed on the lighter weight Sheffield Pullman, but on January 20, 1964 it suffered a serious main generator flashover at speed near Huntington. Back at its builder's works some serious engine problems were discovered, including a cracked sump.

Around the same time BRCW had lost out to Brush Electrical Machines in the battle to win orders for new Type 4s and other business dried up. These financial difficulties meant the facility would close and no more work could be undertaken on *Lion*, bringing the project to a premature end after amassing just 80,000 miles.

Lion's fate was sealed. D0260 was dismantled at AEI's Attercliffe site in Sheffield and the engine was returned to Vickers at Barrow-in-Furness, where it had been built and most probably reused for a Brush Type 4 (Class 47), which uses the same engine. **S**

SULZER POWER 27

FEATURE | BRCW Type 2 (Class 26 and 27)

BRCW's MASTERPIECE Type 2

Originally used in the London area, Birmingham Railway Carriage & Wagon's Type 2 design was to become synonymous with the Scottish Region, where it provided years of excellent service.

The BRCW Type 2 (Class 26 and 27) was developed at the same time as the British Railways version (Class 24 and 25) and utilised the same Sulzer 6LDA28 diesel engine. This certainly helped with maintenances, since the number of power units gave economical scale and reduced the need to train staff on a different engine.

Defining the design
As part of the British Transport Corporation's 1955 Modernisation Plan, BRCW was among the firms awarded a contract to produce some of the pilot locos: 20 diesel electrics in the D11/4 power category (later Type 2s). A partnership between BRCW, Sulzer and Crompton Parkinson had produced several locos for export, and the new model for the UK made considerable use of already established design work.

Construction took place at BRCW's factory in Smethwick, Birmingham. While the body structure was similar to the BR Type 2, its appearance was rather different. The main underframe was of a welded steel type, with two main double channel

28 SULZER POWER
www.railwaysillustrated.co.uk

A typical scene north of the Scottish capital during the 1970s as a pair of Class 26s, 26023 and 26024, approaches the Forth Bridge with an Inverness to Edinburgh service on May 28, 1979. (John Whiteley)

FEATURE | BRCW Type 2 (Class 26 and 27)

Doyen of the Class D5300 awaits repairs at Haymarket in 1968; note that the gangway doors had already been removed and plated over by this time. (Rail Online)

Fresh off the production line, BRCW Type 2 D5332 heads a line-up of three other locos inside Leith station/depot in 1959. (Rail Online)

D5320 and D5344 depart from Nairn with the 1500 Inverness to Glasgow and Edinburgh service on Sunday July 23, 1961. Note the TPO van behind the locos. (John Whiteley)

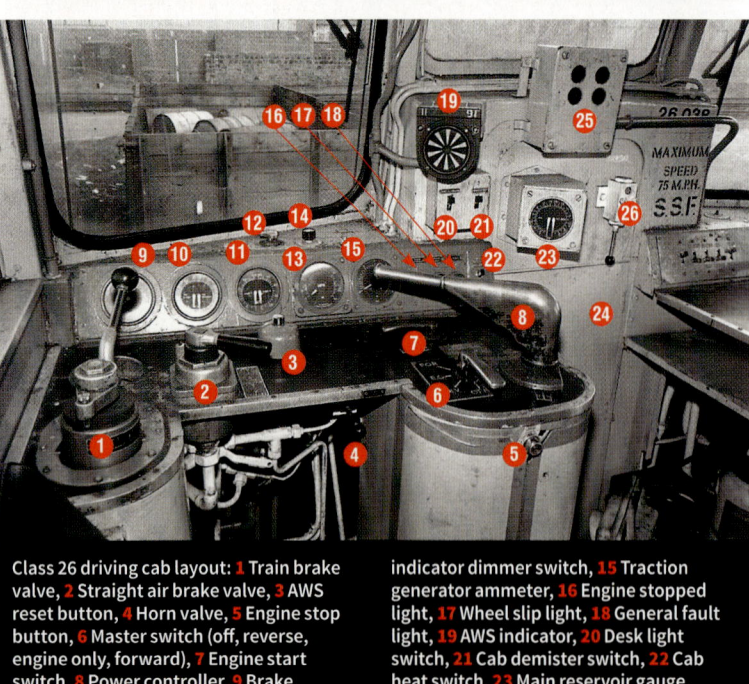

Class 26 driving cab layout: **1** Train brake valve, **2** Straight air brake valve, **3** AWS reset button, **4** Horn valve, **5** Engine stop button, **6** Master switch (off, reverse, engine only, forward), **7** Engine start switch, **8** Power controller, **9** Brake pipe gauge, **10** Vacuum gauge, **11** Brake cylinder gauge, **12** Windscreen wiper control valve, **13** Speedometer, **14** Desk indicator dimmer switch, **15** Traction generator ammeter, **16** Engine stopped light, **17** Wheel slip light, **18** General fault light, **19** AWS indicator, **20** Desk light switch, **21** Cab demister switch, **22** Cab heat switch, **23** Main reservoir gauge, **24** Position of original gangway door, **25** Brake selection indicator, **26** Brake overcharge release valve. (Tom Noble)

longitudinals, which were held in parallel by two transoms at the bogie positions, and two beneath the power unit/generator assembly. The longitudinals contained air cooling ducts for the traction motors, something that was incorporated into the company's subsequent Type 3 (Class 33).

Body design was quite similar to BR's Type 2, in that it used 'I' section vertical and diagonal steel struts to create a lattice-girder to support the underframe and equipment, with Vokes oil-wetted air filters sited in louvres positioned above cant-rail level. Additional filters were placed in the steam heating boiler compartment and large bodyside grills were provided for the radiators that cooled the engine water and lubricating oil (at the No 1 end), with the air drawn through by a roof-mounted, electrically driven and thermostatically controlled fan. Semi-translucent glass-fibre panels were used for the roof and were removable to allow access to the engine and equipment.

As with other designs of the period, gangway connecting doors were provided in the cab fronts to permit crews to move between two locos working in multiple. These quickly became redundant, eventually being removed, and the opening was sealed to eliminate the drafts often complained about by crews.

The 1,160hp variant of the Sulzer 6LDA28 power unit was adopted and was coupled to a Crompton Parkinson main generator. The auxiliary generator was mounted above it for non-traction power. A Stone-Vapour steam heating boiler was provided at the loco's No 2, with its own 100-gallon fuel tank in the same compartment.

Beneath the underframe the loco sat on a pair of equalising beam type bogies fitted with swing bolsters. The bolsters were carried on four suspension links, sprung on both sides with triple elliptical springs, and used rubber stops to limit transverse movement. SKF roller bearings axleboxes were used, while Davies & Metcalfe brake equipment was employed; initially this was air on the loco and vacuum for train braking. The fleet was later equipped with dual air/vacuum brakes.

The bogies housed four nose-suspended 224hp (167kW) Crompton Parkinson series-wound force-ventilated traction motors and were of similar design to those used on the BR Type 4 Peaks and BRCW's later Type 3. The motors were ventilated by a pair of Aerex Hyperform traction motor blowers.

Fuel and water tanks as well as the loco's batteries were positioned between the bogies beneath the underframe, together with appropriate header tanks within the engine room.

Orders and development

Even while the first 20 locos (to become Class 26/0s under TOPS) were under construction, an order for 27 more (Class 26/1) was placed by the BTC. This was followed shortly afterwards by an additional order for 68 of a more powerful variant fitted with the Sulzer 6LDA28-B engine developing 1,250hp (932kW) – identical to the process followed by the BR/Sulzer Type 2s (Classes 24 and 25). As well as being more powerful, the locos, which became Class 27 under TOPS, used GEC electrical

BRCW Type 2 (Class 26 and 27) FEATURE

equipment. A WT981 main generator and a WT782 auxiliary generator were used, along with four WT459 axle-hung nose-suspended traction motors, connected in parallel. These were rated at 236hp (176kW) at 485A, 415V and gave the loco a top speed of 90mph, instead of the 75mph of the original build.

The water and oil pumps took power from the engine starter battery, which meant they continued to provide the necessary oil and water circulation after the engine was shut down. A Stone-Vapour steam heating boiler was used once more, but locos D5370-78 didn't have one as they were originally assigned to North Eastern freight duties. The bogies were a variation on the design used on D5300-46 and had nests of coil springs for secondary suspension, while the bolsters had a shock absorber at each end to overcome vertical riding issues experienced with the original batch. Also addressed was a problem with the traction motor bellows. Improved seating was used to provide constant contact with the ducting to help avoid dirt entering the traction motors.

Externally the most obvious difference was the use of a four-character headcode box above the cab instead of the train description discs used on the earlier locos. Improvements were also made within the cab: reducing drafts from the gangway doors and better positioning of equipment.

Almost new Type 2 D5344 stands outside the old St Rollox shed (65B) on August 12, 1960.
(Gavin Morrison)

Clearly displaying the gangway doors, Type 2 D5323 stops at Gleneagles with a train for Glasgow on August 14, 1965.
(Gavin Morrison)

Into traffic

The first 20 locos began delivery from Smethwick to Doncaster Works (for acceptance) in 1958. They first went to Hornsey Depot in north London for use on King's Cross suburban services, with D5300 arriving at Hornsey on July 29, 1958. Before moving north to Scotland in 1960, the Type 2s provided excellent service on suburban passenger trains from Moorgate and King's Cross, as well as workings to Grimsby and some freight duties.

The second batch of what became Class 26 under TOPS (D5320-46) was allocated directly to the Scottish Region. The first loco was accepted by BR at Doncaster Works in April 1959 and on the 10th it

www.railwaysillustrated.co.uk   SULZER POWER 31

Class 26s 26027 and 26026 head an up special working at Jamestown heading towards Queensferry on April 27, 1985. (Gavin Morrison)

BELOW: With a cattle truck behind the loco, D5328 pauses at Stirling with an Inverness to Glasgow train on August 21, 1964. (John Whiteley)

32 SULZER POWER   www.railwaysillustrated.co.uk

BRCW Type 2 (Class 26 and 27) | **FEATURE**

LEFT: Type 2 D5315 arrives at Edinburgh Waverley with the 0730 from Aberdeen bound for London King's Cross on July 22, 1963. (John Whiteley)

ventured to its new home at Leith, before being allocated to Haymarket Depot shortly afterwards. However, Haymarket's diesel facilities were incomplete, so it remained at Leith for several more months.

Meanwhile, in the London area many of the diesel types from the early pilot order were proving to be problematic and unreliable and as a result the Scottish Region loaned D5330-35 to the Eastern Region in 1959. In Scotland the new engines spent a lot of time being used for crew training, but earned money on passenger turns from Edinburgh to Dundee and Perth, as well as some freight duties. Trials on the route north to Aberdeen took place in 1959, with D5337/8 used to haul 11-coach loads plus a recording vehicle. The following year Inverness Depot received the final 1,160hp locos, D5338-46, while others were transferred to Aberdeen Ferryhill and Perth for training. March 1960 was a significant month as pairs of the Type 2s were introduced on the Edinburgh to Aberdeen route, with a journey time of 3hr 8mins. They remained there until 1962 when EE Type 4s took over. Once the Type 2s originally allocated to the Eastern Region arrived at Haymarket, the Edinburgh depot was able to transfer D5320-37 to Inverness for use on the Highland line, particularly on Glasgow to Aberdeen services.

By 1966 sufficient diesels were available to cover all diagrams and the opportunity was taken to modify the first seven locos, D5300-06, and equip them with slow speed control for working Merry-Go-Round coal trains that served Cockenzie power station. In addition the locos had the steam heat boilers removed and were fitted with dual brakes, since the MGW wagons were air-braked. During the 1970s the loco's ➡

www.railwaysillustrated.co.uk   SULZER POWER 33

FEATURE | BRCW Type 2 (Class 26 and 27)

An Edinburgh to Glasgow Queen Street push-pull service makes a hasty departure from Haymarket on April 20, 1976, with 27201 leading and 27101 bringing up the rear. *(Gavin Morrison)*

air system was upgraded by installing two compressors sourced from withdrawn Class 24s.

The more powerful batch of 1,250hp locos, D5347-D5415, was built in 1961-62 and was divided between three regions. Scotland received D5347-69, the North Eastern Region was allocated D5370-78 at Thornaby Depot, and the London Midland Region took charge of D5379-D5415. The first (D5347) was commissioned for service at Doncaster Works in June 1961 and allocated to Glasgow's Eastfield Depot for use on the West Highland line. The Thornaby-based examples were not equipped with a steam heating boiler as they were to be used on freight diagrams. They remained at the Teesside depot until January 1966 when they were exchanged for the same number of BR/Sulzer Type 2s from the London Midland Region. The LMR already had D5379-D5415, which initially went to Cricklewood Depot in North London. They were mainly used on freight workings, but also powered some suburban services from St Pancras. During 1962 they began hauling St Pancras to Nottingham stopping services in multiple and were occasionally found on the prestigious 'condor' container service between Hendon and Glasgow. Some even put in appearances on the former Great Central route from Marylebone to Nottingham.

The Eastern Region received an example at March Depot in August 1963 when D5403 arrived for crew and fitter training before the type appeared on Toton/LMR to Whitemoor freights. However, by the end of the decade all the Type 2s had moved to Scotland, as BR attempted to standardise traction around the country and confine some designs to specific regions in order to reduce costs. The LMR Type 2s were swapped for Class 20s and 25s, although one, D5383, never made it north of the border as it was withdrawn in January 1966 after it was badly damaged in a collision at East Langton, near Market Harborough on August 20, 1965.

During the long uphill slog heading north, Class 26s D5333 and D5337 make a smoky departure from Blair Atholl with a Perth to Inverness service on March 9, 1973. *(Gavin Morrison)*

26034 passes Haymarket West with the 1248 Edinburgh to Inverness on April 22, 1981. *(Gavin Morrison)*

Class 27/0 27048 approaches Burntisland while working the 1028 Dundee to Edinburgh on August 3, 1984. *(Gavin Morrison)*

BRCW Type 2 (Class 26 and 27) | FEATURE

BRCW Type 2 (Class 26) Technical data

Class	26/0	Class 26/1
Builder:	BRCW	BRCW
Introduced:	1958/59	1959
Number series:	D5300-D5319	D5320-D5346
TOPS number series:	26001-26020	26021-26046
Former class codes:	D11/4, later 11/6	11/6A
Wheel arrangement:	Bo-Bo	Bo-Bo
Route availability:	5 (6 from 1987)	6
Multiple Working:	Blue Star	Blue Star
Engine:	Sulzer 6LDA28A (later B)	Sulzer 6LDA28A (later B)
Horsepower:	1,160hp (865kW)	1,160hp (865kW)
Main generator:	CG391-A1	CG391-A1
Aux generator:	CAG 193-1A	CAG 193-1A
Traction motor type:	CP171-A1	CP171 D3
Brakes (Loco):	Air	Air
Brakes (Train):	Vacuum (later dual)	Vacuum (later dual)
Brake Force:	35 tonnes	35 tonnes
Maximum tractive effort:	42,000lb (186.8kN)	42,000lb (186.8kN)
Power at rail:	900hp (671kW)	900hp (671kW)
Length:	50ft 9in (15.47m)	50ft 9in (15.47m)
Width:	8ft 10in (2.69m)	8ft 10in (2.69m)
Height:	12ft 8in (3.86m)	12ft 8in (3.86m)
Weight:	75-79 tonnes	75-79 tonnes
Wheel diameter:	3ft 7in (1.09m)	3ft 7in (1.09m)
Max speed:	75mph (121km/h)	75mph (121km/h)
Steam Heating:	Stones	Stones
Fuel tank capacity:	500gal (2,275lit)	500gal (2,275lit)
Lub oil capacity:	100gal (455lit)	100gal (455lit)
Boiler water capacity:	550gal (2,502lit)	550gal (2,502lit)

BRCW Type 2 (Class 27) Technical data

Class	27/0	27/1	27/2
Builder:	BRCW	BRCW	BRCW
Introduced:	1961-1962	1970	1974-1975
Number series:	D5347-D5415	From 27/0	From 27/1
TOPS number series:	27001-27066	27101-27124	27201-27212
Former class codes:	D12/3, later 12/6	-	-
Wheel arrangement:	Bo-Bo	Bo-Bo	Bo-Bo
Route availability:	5	5	5
Multiple Working:	Blue Star	Blue Star	Blue Star
Engine:	Sulzer 6LDA28B	Sulzer 6LDA28B	Sulzer 6LDA28B
Horsepower:	1,250hp (932kW)	1,250hp (932kW)	1,250hp (932kW)
Main generator:	GEC WT981	GEC WT981	GEC WT981
Aux generator:	GEC WT782	GEC WT782	GEC WT782
Traction motor type:	GEC WT459	GEC WT459	GEC WT459
Brakes (Loco):	Air	Air	Air
Brakes (Train):	Vacuum/Dual	Dual	Dual
Brake Force:	35 tonnes	35 tonnes	35 tonnes
Maximum tractive effort:	40,000lb (178kN)	40,000lb (178kN)	40,000lb (178kN)
Power at rail:	933hp (696kW)	933hp (696kW)	933hp (696kW)
Length:	50ft 9in (15.47m)	50ft 9in (15.47m)	50ft 9in (15.47m)
Width:	8ft 10in (2.69m)	8ft 10in (2.69m)	8ft 10in (2.69m)
Height:	12ft 8in (3.86m)	12ft 8in (3.86m)	12ft 8in (3.86m)
Weight:	74-77 tonnes	74-77 tonnes	74-77 tonnes
Wheel diameter:	3ft 7in (1.09m)	3ft 7in (1.09m)	3ft 7in (1.09m)
Max speed:	90mph (145km/h)	90mph (145km/h)	90mph (145 km/h)
Heating:	Stones steam	Deutz gen set	Stones electric
Fuel tank capacity:	970gal (4,413lit)	970gal (4,413lit)	970gal (4,413lit)
Lub oil capacity:	100gal (455lit)	100gal (455lit)	100gal (455lit)
Boiler water capacity:	300gal (1,365lit)	-	-

Class 27s dominate this view of Fort William depot on June 5, 1971, with 5360, 5364, 5397, 5401 and 5414 present. (Gavin Morrison)

www.railwaysillustrated.co.uk SULZER POWER 35

FEATURE | BRCW Type 2 (Class 26 and 27)

Push-Pull

The Class 27 is probably best remembered for its use on fast push-pull services between Edinburgh and Glasgow. The Scottish Region was eager to speed up the service and to replace the Swindon-built six-car DMUs that were introduced in the late 1950s. Several classes took part in trials, including Class 37s, 47s and even 50s, but they were in short supply and were needed elsewhere. Rather surprisingly the SCR chose the Class 27 to fulfil the role, working in push-pull fashion at either end of rakes of six original air-braked Mk 2 coaches. Electric train heating was required, together with through locomotive/train engine control and warning systems for safe operation.

To satisfy the requirement, 24 locos and 36 coaches were needed, allowing

Some way from its normal area of operation, Class 26 26025 stands outside the main depot building at Tinsley on September 29, 1987. (Gavin Morrison)

BRCW Type 2 (Class 26 and 27) | FEATURE

Midland Main Line during early 1971. St Rollox Works in Glasgow converted the other 12 locos, although a separate ETH generator set wasn't installed as the existing generator set was modified to supply ETH instead. The new service commenced in May 1971, but almost immediately reliability issues surfaced and various non-push-pull equipped locos stood in. The high-speed running was the cause of most problems and the traction motor bandings had to be strengthened. In addition commutator covers worked loose and sometimes fell off. Modifications were also required to the brake gear and bogie primary coil spring suspension bolts, as well as traction motor suspension. During the autumn of 1971 the constant high-speed running caused ➔

Class 27 27005 inside the former Highland Railway Works at Inverness Depot on April 19, 1986.
(Gavin Morrison)

27049 shunts some tanks at Stirling, probably from either the Cambus Distillers or Menstrie Distillers, on April 8, 1986.
(John Whiteley)

for four locos and one rake of coaches to act as spares. Derby Works undertook the Class 27 modifications, with 12 27/0s arriving from September 1970. The steam heat boiler was removed and a 130kW alternator set powered by a Deutz diesel engine was installed. Dual brakes were added, as was a fully automatic fire-fighting system, which was set to go off if the engine room temperature exceeded 120°C. The traction motors were rewound and the main generator overhauled; the resultant loco was classified as 27/1. Early testing took place on the

www.railwaysillustrated.co.uk

Sulzer Power 37

FEATURE | BRCW Type 2 (Class 26 and 27)

ADB968028 (formerly D5370 and 27024) at Eastfield MPD in June 1988, shortly after its departmental numbers were applied. Official transfer of ownership didn't take place for a further 12 months. The loco is now preserved at the Caledonian Railway. (Stuart Kirkby)

serious vibration in the brush gear and brakes also became a concern. However, the Scottish Region was confident it had overcome most of the issues by the following summer, although generator insulation break-downs and problems with the Deutz alternator sets were on the rise. The pattern of problems continued for the next five years, resulting in Glasgow and Derby Works carrying out numerous repairs and modifications. The push-pull fleet was finally replaced by 47/7s and Mk 3 stock in 1979.

Final years

008/010/025/026/031/032/034/035/037/ 038/040/041). Eight Class 26s later wore Railfreight triple-grey with black cab window surrounds, yellow cab sides and yellow/black Coal Sub sector branding (26001-008) in 1988/89 for use primarily on the Cockenzie coal traffic. There was a further change to 'Dutch' Civil Engineering department grey/yellow livery in 1990-92, which was applied to 16 of the refurbished examples (26001- 008/011/025/026/035/036/038/040/043).

Right at the end of the type's career,

BELOW RIGHT:
Class 26/0 26002 poses beside the servicing building at Eastfield wearing coal sector livery on July 14, 1989. (Gavin Morrison)

Both wearing 'Dutch' engineer's livery, class 26s 26025 and 26026 depart from Oban with a special for Edinburgh on July 12, 1992. (Gavin Morrison)

BRCW Type 2 refurbishment

In 1982, the decision was taken to withdraw the Class 25s but retain the two BRCW Type 2 classes. Both of the latter were showing signs of age, and a heavy general repair or refurbishment programme was sanctioned.

Glasgow's St Rollox Works had been responsible for the majority of major overhauls and modifications to the fleet so far, and was selected to perform the work. Common features were a complete rewiring of the locos, rehabilitation of the electrical machines, a full standard repair of the power unit and bogies, removal of blue asbestos from cab bulkheads and fitting dual train braking equipment where not already done. Fibreglass filter packs were substituted for the original oil-wetted engine room filters.

The A frame in the Sulzer engine in the Class 26s had begun to suffer metal fatigue and the component was replaced with an equivalent from withdrawn Class 25s. Steam heat boilers were also removed.

The Class 27s received the same treatment. However, of those that retained steam generators only three had them removed. The GEC control equipment had never been as reliable as either the Crompton Parkinson or AEI equivalents in the other Sulzer Type 2s. The opportunity was therefore taken during the rewiring of the control cubicle to substitute AEI relays from Class 25s for those of GEC manufacture.

Experience found the refurbished Class 27s to be less reliable due to the work carried out on the control cubicle and so it was cancelled for the remainder of the class after 22 had been dealt with. This meant that all the 33 surviving examples of Class 26 were put through the HGR programme, which was completed by 1987. **David Clough**

BRCW Type 2 (Class 26 and 27) | FEATURE

the two oldest locos were selected for repainting back into 1960s era BR green: D5300 (26007) and D5301 (26001). Obviously small yellow warning panels had to be applied during the repaints at Eastfield, while D5301 was named *Eastfield*, the only member of its class to carry such an embellishment. The locos were rolled out on August 28, 1992 and became instantly popular on the various railtours run in connection with the type's withdrawal.

The Class 27s didn't last as long as their older relatives, which outlasted them by six years. This might seem strange, given the 27s were a little more powerful, but the 27/1s and 27/2s had taken a hammering on the push-pull Edinburgh-Glasgow services during the late 1970s. Afterwards they were put to use on Edinburgh to Dundee semi-fast passenger services and other routes, until they were superseded by Sprinter DMUs in 1987. In the meantime the change of requirements for the locos meant many were converted back to 27/0 specification and renumbered accordingly. Worth noting is the class only ever wore two liveries, BR green and BR blue, with none acquiring any sector colours.

Meanwhile over on the West Highland Line the 27s continued to enjoy plenty of work until they too began to be replaced by new DMUs. The final vacuum brake-only examples were withdrawn by September 1986, leaving just 21 in traffic at Eastfield. In July 1987 all but one of them were withdrawn, with 27008 soldiering on alone until it worked its last train on August 13, with official withdrawal coming on the 19th.

Although not a particularly powerful design, the BRCW Type 2s were popular with crews and maintenance staff, with the spacious engine room making routine maintenance relatively easy. The fleet performed admirably, with a low failure rate, although the push-pull locos did suffer from the intense service they were tasked with.

Fortunately several examples of both classes made their way into preservation and can be seen across the UK at numerous heritage railways, where they continue to provide reliable service. **S**

BELOW LEFT: In immaculate 'Dutch' livery, 26001 basks in the sun at Eastfield depot on May 24, 1991. (Gavin Morrison)

Class 26/27 Survivors

Number	Location	Status
D5301 (26001)	Lakeside & Haverthwaite Railway	Operational
D5302 (26002)	Strathspey Railway	Stored
26004 (D5304)	Burton-upon-Trent	Stored
D5300 (26007)	Barrow Hill	Restoration
D5310 (26010)	Llangollen Railway	Operational
26011 (D5311)	Burton-upon-Trent	Stored
D5314 (26014)	Caledonian Railway	Operational
26024 (D5324)	Bo'ness & Kinneil Railway	Restoration
D5325 (26025)	Strathspey Railway	Stored
26035 (D5335)	Caledonian Railway	Stored
26038 (D5338)	North Yorkshire Moors Railway	Operational
26040 (D5340)	Whitrope Heritage Centre	Restoration
D5343 (26043)	Gloucester Warwickshire Railway	Operational
27001 (D5347)	Bo'ness & Kinneil Railway	Operational
27005 (D5351)	Bo'ness & Kinneil Railway	Restoration
D5353 (27007)	Caledonian Railway	Stored
D5370 (27024)	Caledonian Railway	Operational
D5394 (27050)	Strathspey Railway	Operational
D5401 (27056)	Great Central Railway	Restoration
D5410 (27059)	Cranmore	Restoration
27066 (D5386)	Barrow Hill	Restoration

A sad fate befell many BRCW and BR/Sulzer Type 2s during the 1980s, namely the scrapman's torch. 27023 and 27025 are among those waiting for the chop at Vic Berry's yard on May 8, 1988. (John Stretton)

GREAT SUBSCRIPTION OFFERS FROM

SUBSCRIBE
TO *YOUR* FAVOURITE MAGAZINE
AND SAVE

Sulzer Power

The Railway World – Past, Present and Future

Each issue of Railways Illustrated offers a comprehensive round-up of the latest news and topical events from the UK across the present day railway, including heritage traction in operation on the main lines. Supported by high quality photography and editorial from experienced railway enthusiasts, Railways Illustrated reflects the energy and vitality of the present day railway scene.

www.railwaysillustrated.com

Steam Nostalgia and Railway History at its best

Wherever you live in the British Isles, Steam Days offers nationwide coverage of 'The Days of Steam'. You can be assured of interesting and informative reading in each issue, enhanced with top-quality pictures in colour and black & white and printed to a very high standard.

www.steamdaysmag.co.uk

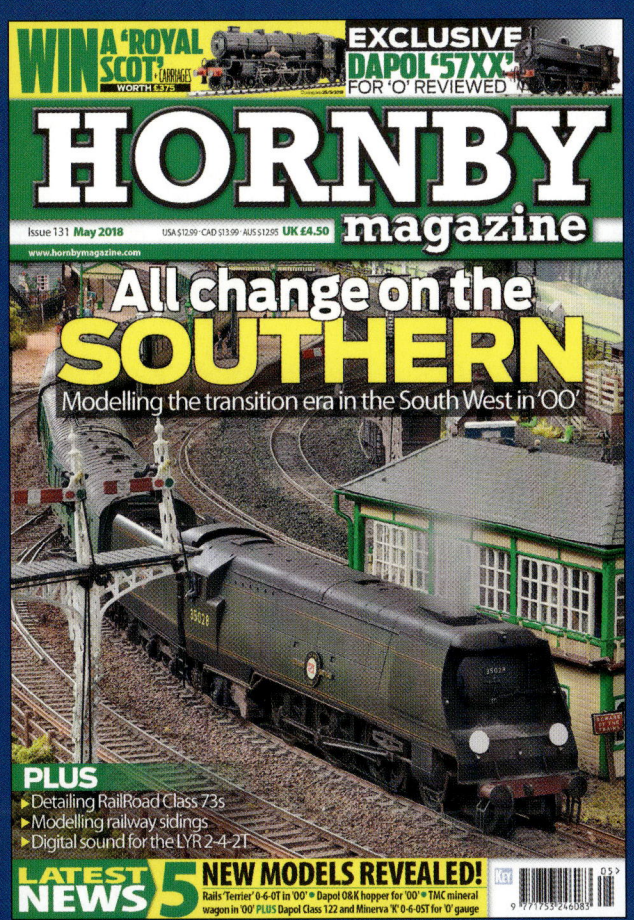
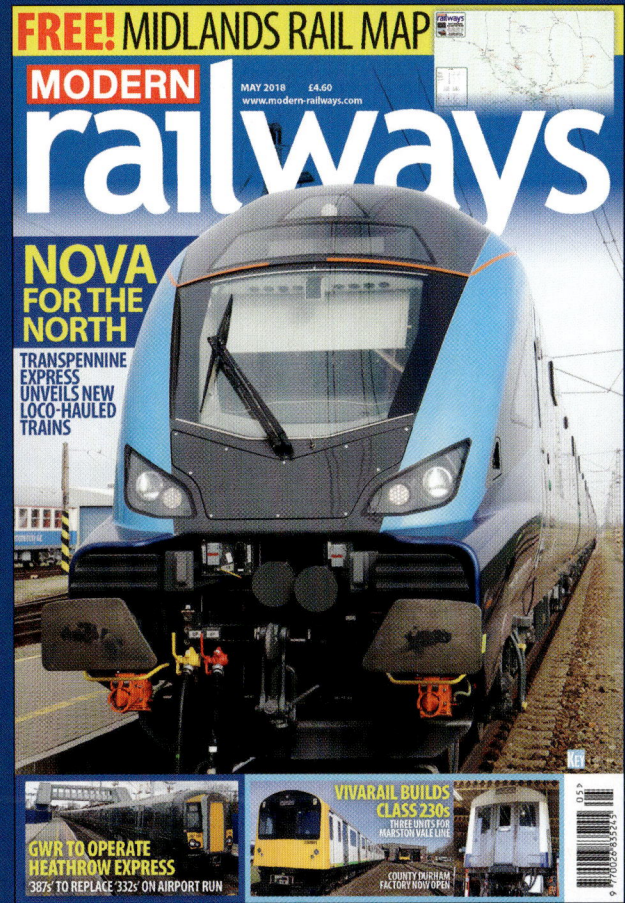

Britain's Fastest Growing Model Railway Magazine...

Hornby Magazine takes a unique approach to model railways with both the relatively inexperienced and the seasoned modeller in mind. Unique step-by-step guides offer modellers hints and tips on how to get the most from the hobby. The very best photography and all the very latest news inspire and inform modellers of all abilities. Hornby Magazine is dedicated to promoting this most rewarding of hobbies, introducing it to newcomers and those returning to the hobby.

www.hornbymagazine.com

News, Views and Analysis on Today's Railway

Established for 50 years, Modern Railways has earned its reputation in the industry as a highly respected railway journal. Providing in-depth coverage of all aspects of the industry, from traction and rolling stock to signalling and infrastructure management, Modern Railways carries the latest news alongside detailed analysis, making it essential reading for industry professionals and railway enthusiasts alike.

www.modern-railways.com

ALSO AVAILABLE DIGITALLY:

 Available on iTunes   Available on the App Store    Available on Google play    Available on BlackBerry    Available on kindle fire   Available on PC, Mac & Windows 10

Available on PC, Mac, Blackberry and Windows 10 from

378/18

FOR THE LATEST SUBSCRIPTION DEALS

VISIT:
www.keypublishing.com/shop

PHONE:
(UK) 01780 480404   (Overseas) +44 1780 480404

FEATURE | Class 33

The Class 33
CROMPTO

Beautifully turned out in BR green, Class 33/0 33008 *Eastleigh* prepares to depart from Waterloo with the Bournemouth Belle railtour on June 21, 1986. (John Whiteley)

Class 33 | FEATURE

NS

Designed to meet the specific needs of the Southern Region, the Birmingham Railway Carriage & Wagon Company Type 3 was an extremely flexible and capable design that outgrew its geographical origins.

The Type 3 power category, covering locos in the 1,500-2,000hp range, was arguably the most flexible of all. As well as providing locos with plenty of power for light and medium freight and passenger work, it also had the ability to haul heavy loads at low to moderate speed. This often obviated the need for running in multiple but, if required, it could provide Type 5 power.

The Birmingham Railway Carriage & Wagon Company was among those chosen to produce a Type 3, and its Class 33s proved to be a successful and popular design. They were originally seen as a replacement for steam on the Southern Region, but in their later years were found more widely across the UK, notably on the Western and Midland Regions, venturing to places such as Cardiff and Crewe. The loco has the honour of being the first UK loco built with electric train heating; it also had duplicate driving controls on both sides of the cab that made shunting, among other things, much easier. Nicknamed 'Cromptons' after the manufacturer of their Crompton Parkinson electrical gear, the type is probably best remembered for the 33/1 variant that worked with 4-TC units between Bournemouth and Weymouth prior to full electrification of the route.

After privatisation many continued to provide stalwart service. Some remain certified for the main line, while plenty made it into preservation.

Concept and design

The 1955 British Transport Commission Modernisation Plan saw a multitude of designs emerge, some more successful than others, but the BRCW Type 2s (later Class 26/27), fitted with a Sulzer 6LDA power unit was among the better examples. In order to meet the BTC's requirement for new Southern Region traction a more powerful version of the BRCW Type 2 was approved. Although the initial preference was for a Co-co bogie layout, a Bo-Bo was argued for on the grounds it would have wider access to the network, and was accepted, along with a top speed of 85mph.

The majority of the design work was performed on the Southern at the Regional M&EE office at London Bridge, with support from the CM&EE Technical Office in Brighton. The result was a visually similar loco to the BRCW Type 2, but equipped with a more powerful Sulzer 8LDA28 engine, rated at 1,550hp (1,156kW). At the time it was the most powerful diesel-electric in the UK running on four axles, with an output of 387.5hp (288kW) per axle.

EMUs, which were all air brake-equipped (either electro pneumatic/automatic or Westinghouse), were quickly dominating the Southern Region. To make the locos compatible they were built with dual (vacuum and air) train brakes from new, assisted by pipe extensions in the engine room to allow couple to waist-level air pipes on the front of EMUs.

BRCW's Type 3 was ordered in several batches. The first batch of 45, in December 1957, was destined for the South Eastern Division. Subsequent orders were for 20 in October 1958, 12 narrow-body variants

FEATURE | Class 33

(Class 33/2) in July 1959 and 21 standard examples in December 1959. The Southern always referred to the locos using a letter-based classification: KA (Class 33/0), KB (Class 33/1) and KC (Class 33/2).

The loco's structure had a welded steel underframe, formed of two main double-channel longitudinals joined by four transoms, with buffers and drawgear attached to a fabricated dragbox on the main underframe. A lattice-girder construction was used for the body, formed out of 'I' section girder steel covered by medium gauge steel plate. Louvres were placed above cant rail height to provide equipment ventilation for the engine and equipment compartment, with the only body side louvres adjacent to the main cooling group at the No 1 end. The removable roof panels were made of translucent reinforced plastics, as were the cab roofs.

The spacious engine room was a single compartment, with the two Reavell vacuum exhausters beside the main cooling group at No 1 end, then the power unit and generator, followed by the main electrical control equipment at the No 2 end housed in a dust-proof compartment. A Metcalfe Oerlikon compressor was mounted in the engine room. Train crews and maintenance staff appreciated the lack of clutter.

The Sulzer 8LDA28 engine was of a turbo-charged design, cooled by a Serck-Behr system incorporating a hydrostatically driven, roof-mounted, thermostatically controlled fan. The Crompton Parkinson generator group was actually three units, one to provide traction power, one was the auxiliary generator providing power for everything except traction and heating, with the third and smallest supplying ETH. When ETH was in use the engine rpm increased from 350rpm to 550rpm.

The cabs were considerably different from the previous BRCW Type 2, most obviously because of the Southern Region-style, two-character headcode panel mounted between the two front windows. No steam heat boiler was fitted; instead the use of ETH was adopted. This saved a lot of weight and was available simply at the touch of a button, provided the stock was compatible.

The traction motors comprised four Crompton Parkinson Cl71 C2s, with a continuous rating of 305hp, which were series wound, force-ventilated, axle hung and nose-suspended. The same company supplied the two traction motor blowers, which were mounted in the main engine compartment, one for each bogie. The bogies were based on those fitted to the BRCW Type 2 and were of the equalising-beam type with swing bolsters. They were made of mild steel plate formed into box sections and the primary bolster was supported on four suspension links and sprung at both sides. The bogie spring planks were cast steel and each was supported on two links from cross bars. Four nests of coil springs held the bogie frame on to the equalising beam. The SKF axleboxes used roller bearings. As with other Type 2s the fuel tank and roll-out battery boxes were fitted beneath the underframe between the bogies.

ABOVE: A yet to be modified BRCW Type 3, D6511 (later 33101), hauls a 4-TC set through Basingstoke on September 24, 1966. (Gavin Morrison)

BELOW: BRCW Type 3 D6577 approaches Basingstoke with a down freight on September 24, 1966. (Gavin Morrison)

Build and introduction

All of the BRCW Type 3s were built at the firm's Smethwick Works between February 1959 and May 1962. Once finished the locos were generally delivered to the SR under their own power and were commissioned at Hither Green. Although consideration was given to constructing the whole fleet to fit narrow tunnels on the Tonbridge to Hastings route, the complexities of designing the locos for this purpose would have taken too long, delaying production. It was decided to build the final 12 to the Hastings load gauge, seven inches narrower than standard. Although this might have seemed an easy job, in fact it required considerable redesign and cost BRCW dearly, and was one reason why it abandoned building main line locos.

The first BRCW Type 3, D6500, was rolled out in November 1959 and was delivered to Hither Green on December 17, with trial running in Kent commencing in March 1960. Electrification of the Chatham route to Dover and the Kent Coast took place in June 1959. Prior to that, diesel requirements were satisfied by the loan of 15 BR/Sulzer Type 2s from the London Midland Region. Subsequent

44 SULZER POWER

Class 33 | FEATURE

ABOVE: Class 33/0 33025 passes Salisbury Tunnel Jn with an up service for Waterloo on June 1, 1979. (Gavin Morrison)

RIGHT: BRCW Type 3 D6575 passes through Doncaster with the Uddingston to Cliffe cement empties on May 14, 1963. (John Whiteley)

commissioning took place at Hither Green, along with test runs using passenger stock between Hither Green and Dover.

Sufficient Type 3s were available by the summer of 1960 to permit most Charing Cross to Dover trains to be diesel-hauled while Stage 2 of the electrification work continued. Type 2s had to be used with the Type 3s to provide steam heating in the winter of 1962/63 because the rolling stock was only steam heat-equipped. However, during summer weekends and bank holidays they replaced steam 'H' Class 0-4-4Ts on Gravesend to Allhallows trains formed of vintage pre-grouping push-pull sets.

BRCW Type 3 (Class 33) Technical data

Class:	33/0	33/1	33/2
Builder:	BRCW	BRCW	BRCW
Introduced:	1960-1962	1965-1966	1962
Number series:	D6500-D6585	Random	D6586-D6597
TOPS number series:	33001-33065	33101-33119	33201-33212
Former class codes:	D15/1, later 15/6	D15/2, later 15/6A	
Wheel arrangement:	Bo-Bo	Bo-Bo	Bo-Bo
Route availability:	6	6	6
Multiple Working:	Blue star	Blue star	Blue star
Engine:	Sulzer 8LDA28A	Sulzer 8LDA28A	Sulzer 8LDA28A
Horsepower:	1,550hp (1,156kW)	1,550hp (1,156kW)	1,550hp (1,156kW)
Main generator:	CG391-B1	CG391-B1	CG391-B1
Aux generator:	CAG193-A1	CAG193-A1	CAG193-A1
ETH Generator:	CAG392-A1	CAG392-A1	CAG392-A1
Traction motor type:	C171-C2	C171-C2	C171-C2
Brakes (Loco):	Air	Air	Air
Brakes (Train):	Dual	Dual	Dual
Brake force:	35 tonnes	35 tonnes	35 tonnes
Maximum tractive effort:	45,000lb (200kN)	45,000lb (200kN)	45,000lb (200kN)
Power at rail:	1,215hp (909kW)	1,215hp (909kW)	1,215hp (909kW)
Length:	50ft 9in (15.47m)	50ft 9in (15.47m)	50ft 9in (15.47m)
Width:	9ft 3in (2.81m)	9ft 3in (2.81m)	8ft 8in (2.64m)
Height:	12ft 8in (3.86m)	12ft 8in (3.86m)	12ft 8in (3.86m)
Weight:	77 tonnes	78 tonnes	77 tonnes
Wheel diameter:	3ft 7in (1.09m)	3ft 7in (1.09m)	3ft 7in (1.09m)
Max speed:	85mph (137km/h)	85mph (137km/h)	85mph (137km/h)
Fuel tank capacity:	750gal (3,410lit)	750gal (3,410lit)	750gal (3,410lit)
Lub oil capacity:	108gal (491lit)	108gal (491lit)	108gal (491lit)

The cab layout of Class 33/0 33007: **1** Sanding valve, **2** Exhauster speed-up button, **3** Straight air brake valve, **4** Auto train brake valve, **5** Windscreen wiper valve, **6** AWS reset button, **7** Horn valve, **8** Master switch (off, reverse, engine only, forward), **9** Master key socket, **10** Power controller, **11** Engine start button, **12** Engine stop button, **13** Route indicator light switch, **14** Instrument panel light switch, **15** Engine running light, **16** Wheelslip warning light, **17** Fault light, **18** Driver's side cab heat, **19** Secondman's side cab heat, **20** Demister switch, **21** Main reservoir and brake pipe pressure gauge, **22** Brake cylinder pressure gauge, **23** Vacuum gauge, **24** Speedometer, **25** Amp meter, **26** AWS indicator, **27** Headcode blind controller, **28** Train heat 'on' button and **29** Parking brake. (Colin Marsden Collection)

SULZER POWER 45

FEATURE | Class 33

Meanwhile Type 3s began to dominate freight traffic in Kent and from February 1961 they handled all freight, including the Hundred of Hoo branch, including the cement traffic from Cliffe and oil trains from the Grain refinery. The electrified lines between Sevenoaks and Dover went live on June 12, 1961 and EMUs took over passenger duties. The Type 3s and some Type 2s were deployed onto other non-electrified routes, such as Maidstone East to Ashford and Ashford to Ramsgate, as well as those not being electrified, such as Ashford to Hastings/New Romney. By October 1961, Stage 2 electrification was completed and, helped by more EMU deliveries, the Type 2s returned to the LMR while the Type 3s became confined to freight and parcels duties.

Although Class 50s tended to dominate the Waterloo to Exeter service during the 1980s, Class 33s also found plenty of work to the Devon city. A good example is 33061, leaving Exeter Central with the 1358 Exeter St Davids to Brighton on March 8, 1980.
(John Whiteley)

33055 and 33049 smoke their way through Salisbury with an Amey Roadstone train on November 27, 1982.
(John Whiteley)

Push-Pull

As part of the Southern Region's modernisation plan for the Bournemouth/Weymouth route, it was decided in 1965 that there was a requirement for push-pull traction where a loco could be marshalled at one end of a multiple unit formation, but controlled from a remote driving cab. To meet the need, Type 4 D6580 was fitted with high-level air pipes and control jumpers at Eastleigh Works in June 1965. Successful testing was undertaken with a specially formed six-coach trailer control set between Wimbledon and Basingstoke.

With plans to only electrify as far as Bournemouth, a decision was taken to convert 18 further standard BRCW Type 3s (Class 33/1) and fit TC (trailer control) equipment. The 18 differed from D6580 by having drop-head buckeye couplers, retractable buffers and a centre rubbing plate; these were later added to D6580. The push-pull equipment allowed the Type 3s to be marshalled in any position within a train of 1963/66 EMU stock and controlled from any other cab. Primarily they were used to convey 4-TC units between Bournemouth and Weymouth, taking over from the 4-REP powered EMUs at Bournemouth on the southbound journey.

Flexibility

BRCW's Type 3s were fitted with Blue Star (electro-pneumatic) multiple working cabling from new, meaning they could work with any loco equipped with the same system. This included classes 20, 25, 26, 27, 31, 37 and the SR's Class 73 electro-diesels when working on diesel power.

Few changes were made to the fleet in terms of equipment, although the Class 33/2 'Slim Jim' locos were fitted with

Class 33 | FEATURE

The contrast between the Class 33/0 (33004 right) and the 33/1 fitted with waist level pipes and connections for working with EMUs (33113 left) is apparent as the two stand in the Eastleigh Depot carriage sidings on March 7, 1982. (Gavin Morrison)

slow-speed control from 1971 to allow them to be used on merry-go-round duties. Colour schemes used included BR green when built and BR blue from the mid-1960s. The first real change came in 1982 when Eastleigh painted 33012 with wrap-round yellow cab ends, but this was short-lived. When BR's naming policy was relaxed in the late 1970s several locos were named, which continued until withdrawal.

During the type's early years a couple of locos were involved in specific tests. One example, D6504, was loaned to BR's Derby Research Centre for electric train heat tests and development work. It took part in static load bank tests at Derby and dynamic runs between Derby and Hornsey via Peterborough and the East Coast Main Line between Hornsey, King's Cross and Edinburgh Craigentinny on February 14-17, 1961. In 1964, D6553 visited Derby as part of air brake trials in connection with the development of the Freightliner concept.

Later in life, Class 33/1 33115 was modified as part of the development of retractable bogie-mounted third rail power collection shoes for the proposed Eurostar fleet. The loco was earmarked for disposal at Eastleigh on May 10, 1989. The modification contract was performed by RFS Engineering, Doncaster and the loco arrived at its facility on May 27. The engine and internal equipment were retained, but in an inoperable condition. A new design of unpowered bogie, with two retractable power collection slippers on each side, was fitted and the loco repainted in mainline livery. As the vehicle was unpowered it was classified as a DVT and renumbered to 83301. During the tests it was semi-permanently coupled to

Class 33/1 'Bagpipe' 33113 leaves Clapham Junction with the 1010 Waterloo to Salisbury service on April 8, 1989. (John Whiteley)

www.railwayillustrated.co.uk · Sulzer Power 47

FEATURE | Class 33

A pair of Class 33/0s, 33029 and 33013, approach Acton with a loaded Marcon aggregates working on March 8, 1989. (John Whiteley)

In their later years the Class 33s worked even further afield, even reaching Manchester. Class 33/0 33030 waits to depart Manchester Piccadilly with an afternoon service to Cardiff on April 27, 1986. (Gavin Morrison)

Class 73/2 73205. It moved to the RTC Derby on February 20, 1990, and then to Stewarts Lane and North Pole depots from where extensive testing was performed. Its final test run was on May 5, 1994. It was subsequently moved to St Leonards Depot for storage and was broken up in July 1996.

Active service

Following the completion of the Kent electrification project the Type 3s began to spread their wings wider across the SR. The narrow KC variant remained mostly confined to duties on the Tonbridge to Hastings line, although they could appear anywhere in the South Eastern Division.

One of the most amazing duties by a BRCW Type 3 was its use on the 0230 Cliffe (Holborough) to Uddingston cement train, which ran along the ECM to York from December 1961. The train loaded to 28 four-wheel tank wagons and was initially double-headed. However, it was soon established that a single loco could handle the job, making it one of the most extraordinary inter-regional diagrams at the time.

Eastleigh was later widely associated with the Types 3s, but they first arrived at the depot in July 1962 when a dozen were transferred there to help haul oil traffic from the Fawley refinery. In all, the Types 3s took over seven diagrams from steam traction, including some that used the Didcot, Newbury and Southampton line as far as Didcot, as well as a turn that took them to Southall with a train for Denham. At the same time, the Eastleigh locos assumed a passenger role, working the 0722 to Waterloo (the Le Havre boat train), the 1130 Waterloo-Bournemouth and 1655 return, as well as the 2235 Waterloo to Weymouth mail train. By

48 SULZER POWER

www.railwaysillustrated.co.uk

Class 33 | FEATURE

February 1963 the South Western Division was using its new diesels extensively and rosters covered the area between Nine Elms, Reading, Salisbury, Southampton, Portsmouth and Chichester.

Moving slightly east to the Central Division, the Type 3s, still based at Hither Green, began appearing on freight and some passenger duties, including several peak-hour trains on the Oxted line in May 1963. Steam was used during the winter, but soon ETH-fitted stock was transferred from elsewhere to allow the Type 3s to run year-round. The same summer saw up to 20 examples regularly assigned to Central Division freight and passenger work. At the same time the South Western Division acquired a further 11 examples, allowing more services, including those to Lymington Pier and Swanage, to say goodbye to steam.

In December 1963, the Fawley-Bromford Bridge oil tank train, at the time the heaviest on BR, was re-routed from the Didcot, Newbury, Southampton line and ran to a faster schedule thanks to the use of a pair of Type 3s. In September 1964 the Waterloo to West of England services were taken over by Western Region Type 4 Warship diesel-hydraulics, although Type 3s would soon get their chance. By the end of that year the Type 3s were allocated to Eastleigh (27), Hither Green (58) and St Leonards (12).

South Western Type 3s were soon

ABOVE: A late afternoon commuter service, the 1638 to Yeovil Junction, departs Waterloo on April 15, 1983 behind 33034. (John Whiteley)

FAR LEFT: Although originally built for the restricted clearances on the Tonbridge to Hastings route, the 'Slim Jim' Class 33/2s were later found wandering more widely on the BR network. A good example is 33212 as it passes Severn Tunnel Junction with the 1210 Cardiff to Portsmouth on July 9, 1986. (John Whiteley)

diagrammed for the Saturday 1100 Waterloo to Exeter service, but they were also called upon to deputise for the diesel-hydraulics. However, in late 1965 the production JB electro-diesels (Class 73/1) began to appear and they rapidly took over diesel turns on electrified routes on the Central and South Eastern Divisions. In turn this allowed more Type 3s to move to the South Western Division and in the summer of 1966 virtually all Sunday Waterloo to Bournemouth trains were diesel-hauled to facilitate diversion via the steeply graded Mid-Hants or Portsmouth Direct double-headed.

Delivery of the 4-TC sets for use on the Waterloo to Weymouth route began to arrive in August 1966. From November they also served Salisbury and Basingstoke. To begin with the sets were hauled in the standard way, but when the first KB Type 3, D6521, was delivered, a diagram utilising it in push-pull mode with the 4-TCs began in December 1966, working the 0930 from Waterloo.

On April 3, 1967 the 'juice' became live as far as Bournemouth, allowing the 4-TCs to be hauled/propelled by either an electro-diesel or the new 4-REP units. From July 10, the full service was introduced, with the Type 3s powering the trains from Bournemouth to Weymouth and back. The Type 3/4-TC combination was also deployed on other duties, including some commuter services and between Clapham Junction and Kensington Olympia.

www.railwaysillustrated.co.uk Sulzer Power 49

FEATURE | Class 33

Class 33 survivors

Number	Location	Status
D6501 (33002)	South Devon Railway	Operational
D6508 (33008)	Battlefield Line	Overhaul
D6515 (33012)	Swanage Railway	Operational
33018	Mangapps Railway Museum	Restoration
33019	Battlefield Line	Restoration
33021	Churnet Valley Railway	Restoration
33025	Carnforth (WCR)	Main line
33029	Carnforth (WCR)	Main line
33030	Carnforth (WCR)	Stored
33035	Barrow Hill	Operational
33046	East Lancashire Railway	Stored unserviceable
D6566 (33048)	West Somerset Railway	Operational
D6570 (33052)	Kent & East Sussex Railway	Stored unserviceable
33053	Mid-Hants Railway	Operational
D6575 (33057)	West Somerset Railway	Operational
D6583 (33063)	Spa Valley Railway	Operational
D6585 (33065)	Spa Valley Railway	Restoration
6513 (33102)	Churnet Valley Railway	Restoration
33103	Ecclesbourne Valley Railway	Operational
33108	Severn Valley Railway	Operational
33109	East Lancashire Railway	Operational
33110	Bodmin & Wenford Railway	Operational
33111	Swanage Railway	Operational
D6535 (33116)	Great Central Railway	Operational
6536 (33117)	East Lancashire Railway	Restoration
33201	Swanage Railway	Operational
33202	Mangapps Railway Museum	Operational
33207	Carnforth (WCR)	Main line
D6593 (33208)	Battlefield Line	Restoration

In 1976 Class 33/4-TC diagrams provided an hourly service between Reading and Portsmouth. During the 1980s, the Class 33s proved a valuable asset during winter weather by hauling EMUs through snow and ice, and were also used on the Shepperton Branch, which often suffered flooding in Fulwell Cutting. The Class 71 to 74 conversion programme ran behind schedule and so Cromptons continued to be deployed on some Waterloo to Weymouth and Swanage services after 1967. They were also a regular sight on the Weymouth Quay line, powering the Channel Islands boat express from Bournemouth from 1973.

South coast services between Brighton and Exeter were regular Class 33 turns between 1968 and 1971, and from 1977, while during the early 1970s they appeared at Bristol and Cardiff with summer extras. They continued to power much of the Fawley oil traffic, even making it to Plymouth and Tiverton Junction.

The class became a frequent visitor to Exeter from October 4, 1971, when it took over services from Waterloo following the withdrawal of the WR's Warships. However, with less power available, train lengths were reduced to eight coaches in winter and nine in summer; however, timings were also relaxed by ten minutes. The class became an established sight in Devon, with the Waterloo stock usually stabled at Newton Abbott overnight, and from 1975 an additional turn saw a Class 33

Only two Class 33s wore the Network SouthEast livery – 33035 and 33114. The latter is at the rear of a shuttle service between Bournemouth West Depot and the station during an open day on September 12, 1992. (Gavin Morrison)

50 SULZER POWER   www.railwaysillustrated.co.uk

Class 33 | FEATURE

LEFT: As far north as the class ever reached, 33116 and 33109 head for the fuelling point at Inverness before heading south towards London with a railtour on April 1, 1995.
(Gavin Morrison)

NEXT LEFT: Probably substituting for a Class 50, 33011 and 33029 pass Vauxhall with the 0910 Waterloo to Exeter St Davids service on October 1, 1988.
(John Whiteley)

FAR LEFT: 33030 stands in Guild Street Yard, Aberdeen (now a supermarket) on May 31, 2000 and was the only member of the class to receive EWS colours.
(Gavin Morrison)

BELOW: In 'Dutch' livery, 33208 and 33009 enter Sonning Cutting with ballast empties for Meldon on August 29, 1991.
(John Whiteley)

working to Barnstaple from Exeter.
Another feather in the cap for the Crompton was working cross-country services from Poole and Southampton as far as Reading, where a Class 47 usually took over. If one was not available they often continued as far as Birmingham New Street. The SR revived the 'Pleasure seeker' excursions in the mid-1970s and quite remarkably the class ventured to a host of unusual destinations, including Derby, Evesham, Hereford, Norwich, Paignton and Spalding. It also had some double-headed freightliner duties to Willsden and Birmingham Lawley Street as well as more Fawley oil traffic.
From May 1980, units on the Portsmouth to Bristol route were replaced entirely by Class 33s and coaches, while Class 50s took over the Exeter to Waterloo route. However, additional trains between Waterloo and Salisbury were provided by Cromptons and 4-TCs or coaches. Further work started in 1981 when the class took over more inter-regional trains to Cardiff and Weston-super-Mare. In June the same year, Class 33s replaced Class 25s on Cardiff to Crewe service and they even powered parcel trains between Crewe and Stoke-on-Trent and from Cardiff to Gloucester.
With a reduced requirement on the SR, Class 33s began venturing even further afield, reaching West Wales in May 1982 with six daily three-day cyclic Eastleigh diagrams reaching Swansea, Fishguard Harbour and Milford Haven. On the down side the majority of cross-country services were by now Class 47/4 turns. Another train to regularly have Class 33 power during the 1980s was the VSOE Pullman.
Amazingly, the use of Class 33s on the West Highland line was considered, although in the end ETH-fitted Class 37s got that job. Something extraordinary that did occur was the diagramming of the class for regional services to Manchester and Holyhead!
It still found favour during the years of sectorisation prior to privatisation and this resulted in them appearing in a wide range of liveries. Group Standard headlights were fitted centrally on the front end during the 1990s. After privatisation EWS took on some Cromptons, although they were not part of its long-term planning. However, 33025 and 33030 were given a light overhaul and transferred to Inverness to work local trips, which ran between the end of 1999 and January 2001.
The class was also used by Direct Rail Services, FM Rail and West Coast Railways; the latter still has a couple main line registered. Fortunately the preservation world has been kind to the class, with 24 examples surviving.
Considering the loco was designed specifically to meet the needs of the Southern Region, it is remarkable that it went on to work across a much wider geographical area, demonstrating not only the robustness of the design, but also the flexibility of the Type 3 power group. **S**

FEATURE | Class 44-46

In unfamiliar surroundings, Class 44 44004 *Great Gable* (minus its nameplates), comes off the avoiding line at Holgate Bridge Jn, York, with an up coal train on April 11, 1978.
(John Whiteley)

Class 44-46 | **FEATURE**

Heavyweight Type 4s
THE PEAKS

Initially ten of the British Railways-built Type 4s were ordered as part of the modernisation scheme pilot locos. Eventually almost 200 were built for the Eastern, Midland and Western Regions.

FEATURE | Class 44-46

As part of the British Transport Commission's 1955 modernisation plan, there was a requirement for a Type 4 locomotive. In response, English Electric produced its version, later designated the Class 40, but another solution was offered by British Railways itself using a 12-cylinder Sulzer power unit. Among the 174 pilot scheme locos ordered were ten BR/Sulzer Type 4s, numbered D1-D10, developing 2,300hp. They were named after English and Welsh mountains and hills, and it was no surprise that they were quickly dubbed the 'Peaks'. Subsequent follow-on orders (Class 45 and 46) were also known by the same nickname, despite none of them actually being officially named as such.

The first ten

The ten locos ordered by the BTC were fitted with a Sulzer 12LDA28A power unit rated at 2,300hp (1,715kW) and Crompton Parkinson electrical equipment. British Railways' Derby Works was contracted to build them in late 1957 and the original concept envisaged the use of three axle bogies. The construction methods used at the time meant the axle weight couldn't be kept below the 20 ton maximum stipulated, so a 1Co-Co1 bogie arrangement, the same as on the EE Type 4, was used instead.

Work commenced on the first two locos in August 1958, with the first, D1 *Scafell Pike*, making an appearance in March 1959. The following month it underwent initial testing in the Derby area before venturing to London St Pancras for a BTC inspection on April 21. Further attention was given at Derby before it was officially handed over to Derby shed (17A) on August 11. Rather unusually, all ten pilot locos were delivered with their nameplates already attached, although only D1 received any ceremony – which took place at Carlisle on July 14, 1959.

The pioneering engine left Derby shed shortly after it arrived, transferring to Camden shed just north of London Euston for use on West Coast Main Line services, although it was closely monitored by Derby technicians.

The last of the pilot scheme order (D10) was delivered on February 6, 1960 and it joined the rest on WCML services, where crews were being trained at Carlisle Upperby, Crewe North, Liverpool Edge Hill and Longsight in Manchester. The small fleet only worked on the WCML until 1962, when they were all transferred to Toton where they would remain for the rest of their careers. With the TOPS system due to be introduced in the early 1970s, all BR locos were classified under a new numbering system, and the ten pilot scheme Peaks became Class 44.

Class 45 and 46

As with several other pilot scheme designs a larger production order was placed for more of the Type 4s, even before D1 had turned a wheel. The BTC placed orders for 127 examples (D11 to D137, which became Class 45), fitted with an updated and uprated 12LDA28 B power plant. A third order for 76 locos (later Class 46) was made in →

54 SULZER POWER   www.railwaysillustrated.co.uk

Class 44-46 | **FEATURE**

ABOVE: D1 *Scafell Pike* leaves the paint shop, the final job before main line testing, on April 21, 1959 as the workers who built her admire their handiwork. (John Tidmarsh)

TOP LEFT: The very first Peak, D1 *Scafell Pike*, and Type 2 D5015 near completion in the brand-new finishing shop at Derby Works on April 13, 1959. (John Tidmarsh)

LEFT: Type 4 Peak D15 climbs Shap at Bessygill with the up Waverley, diverted from the Settle to Carlisle route, presumably because of engineering works, on June 11, 1962. (John Whiteley)

Sulzer Power 55

FEATURE | Class 44-46

D113 illustrates a slightly different type of headcode arrangement; a central headcode box, but divided into two halves. It is approaching Leeds City with the 3N11 0440 Derby to Leeds City parcels on February 19, 1963. (John Whiteley)

Destined to become a Class 46 under TOPS, D183 (46046) heads south through Selby, with the up 'Flying Scotsman' on December 13, 1962. (John Whiteley)

Most Peaks were supposed to be built at Derby, however, its workload was such that a considerable number of what became Class 45s were actually assembled at Crewe Works instead. The Sulzer engine and generator assembly is lowered into D101 (45061) at Crewe in early 1961. (Colin Marsden collection)

Class 44-46 | FEATURE

Peak Survivors

Number	Location	Status
D4	Midland Railway Centre – Butterley	Operational
D8	Peak Rail	Operational
45015 (D14)	The Battlefield Line	Stored
45041 (D53)	Midland Railway Centre – Butterley	Operational
45060 (D100)	Barrow Hill	Operational
45105 (D86)	Barrow Hill	Under restoration
45108 (D120)	Midland Railway Centre – Butterley	Operational
45112 (D61)	Burton upon Trent	Stored
45118 (D67)	Barrow Hill	Under restoration
D123 (45125)	Great Central Railway	Operational
45132 (D22)	Epping Ongar Railway	Under restoration
45133 (D40)	Midland Railway Centre – Butterley	Operational
45135 (D99)	East Lancs Railway	Stored
45149 (D135)	Gloucester Warwickshire Railway	Operational
46010 (D147)	Great Central Railway – Nottingham	Under restoration
46035 (D172)	Crewe Heritage Centre	Stored
D182 (46045)	Midland Railway Centre – Butterley	Operational

Peak D175 (46038) departs from Leeds Central with the up Yorkshire Pullman on February 19, 1963. (John Whiteley)

SULZER POWER 57

FEATURE | Class 44-46

1958 and they differed by having Brush electrical equipment instead of Crompton Parkinson. However, when BR and Brush began development of a Co-Co Type 4 (which became the Class 47), the final 20 of the last Peak order were not built, with the equipment used instead on the new BR design.

Design and differences

Visually, the shape of the Peak classes was identical. There were a lot of minor detail differences, but the greatest was the adoption of different style nose ends. This came about as practical requirements changed along with the method of displaying train reporting designations. The first ten locos were fitted with gangway doors and train reporting discs, as already used by steam locos. By the time the production locos were built, things had changed: D11-31 and D68-107 retained the gangway doors, but were fitted with headcode boxes on either side of it, each able to display two characters of the train reporting number using roller blinds. The remaining locos, D32-67 and all those numbered above D108, had no gangway doors and were equipped with a centrally mounted four-character headcode box.

Even the latter became redundant in the mid-1970s when the requirement to show the train reporting number was dropped. Gradually all the headcode boxes were removed, with the nose end sealed and marker lights installed instead. In addition a high intensity headlight was added during the 1980s.

With its workshop number 7-1 displayed on the headcode blinds, Type 4 D114 (45066) is lowered onto its wheelsets at Crewe Works in July 1961. Most loco types were lifted using four single points of contact, but Peak bodies were mounted in the frame lifting brackets illustrated. (Colin Marsden collection)

Not a normal duty for a Peak, the up Yorkshire Pullman waits to depart Leeds Central behind D169 (46032) on April 15, 1967. (Gavin Morrison)

58 SULZER POWER www.railwaysillustrated.co.uk

Class 44-46 | FEATURE

ABOVE: Class 44 original Peak 44010 *Tryfan* stands in front of the huge motive power depot at Toton on July 8, 1976. Along with 44009, it was fitted with different style bodyside grills. (Gavin Morrison)

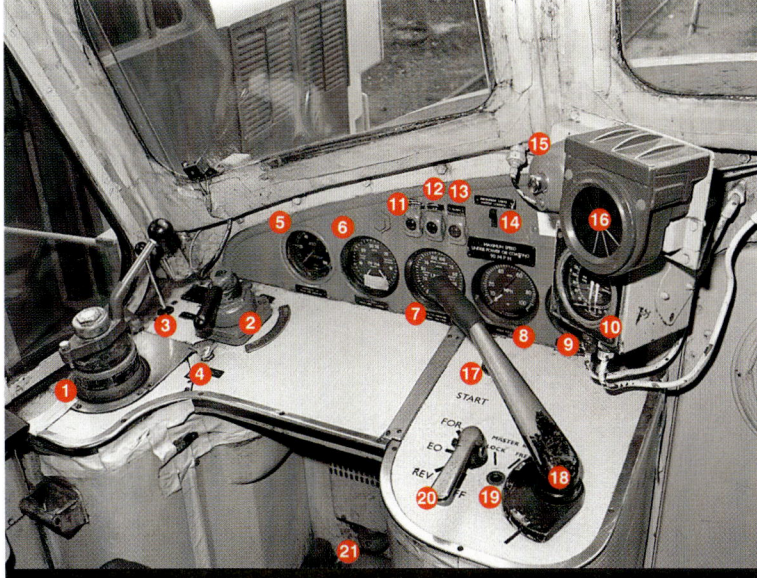

A Class 45 cab depicting the driver's position: **1** Train brake valve, **2** Straight air brake valve, **3** Warning horn valve, **4** Windscreen wiper valve, **5** Train pipe air, **6** Vacuum gauge, **7** Brake cylinder pressure gauge, **8** Speedometer, **9** Main generator ammeter, **10** Main reservoir pressure gauge, **11** Engine stopped warning light (red), **12** Wheelslip light (amber), **13** Fault light (blue), **14** Panel light switch, **15** AWS re-set button, **16** AWS indicator, **17** Start switch, **18** Power controller, **19** Key socket, **20** Master switch, **21** DSD pedal. (Colin Marsden collection)

Construction

To satisfy the axle loading of no more than 20 tons, the 1Co-Co1 bogie used on all Peaks was developed from the type employed on the earlier Southern Region English Electric powered diesel electrics, 10201-10203. Stronger springing was incorporated on the Peaks as they weighed considerably more than the SR prototypes. The leading guide axle on each bogie was mounted in a separate pony truck within the main bogie frame and was guided using side springs. It was also linked to the buffer beam.

Several issues with cracking affected the bogies during the Peak's careers, notably at the top of the side members behind the first cross stay. Initially any cracked bogies were immediately replaced, but things changed over the years and by the 1980s it wasn't until a crack measured three inches that the bogie was swapped or repaired. Efforts were made to prevent fractures and in the mid-1970s a Class 45 was fitted with Flexicoil pivots on the pony truck, which was also modified to allow it to swing from a central pivot. Furthermore, to limit the bogies to a curve radius of five chains, rotational stops and side control blocks were fitted. These were also discovered to cause bogie frame fractures and were removed as a consequence. Afterwards the bogies could safely negotiate curves down to a radius of three and a half chains.

No other major issues were reported and the bogies generally gave good reliable service, although there were small problems that never went away, such as small defects that could cause rough riding at speed.

The bogies could be used under any version of the Type 4. This only changed when the ETH-equipped Class 45/1 appeared in the 1970s because they had additional electrical conduits and no steam heating fittings, meaning they could not be used on the Class 44, 45/0s or 46s. The loco's batteries were fitted below the underframe between the bogies.

Above the bogies, the frame was formed of two longitudinal members connected by several cross beams to form a strong multi-box section; the bogie centres were mounted on two of the cross members.

Bridge girder construction was adopted with diagonal welded bracing struts supporting the body sides to the frame section and curved cross-members joining the two body side frames at cantrail height. The stressed steel construction method was used for the body sides, with a single large grille covering several ventilation holes. This was done to avoid the multiple grilles as used on the BR/Sulzer Type 2. Two of the pilot order, D9 and D10 had vertical ribbing on the grilles instead of the horizontal style used on the rest of the fleet. Unlike most other locos of the period there were no engine room windows or doors. Some auxiliary equipment, including the ➔

BELOW: At the time allocated to Bristol Bath Road, Peak D34 (45119) takes on water for its train heating boiler at Leeds City during 1967. (Rail Photoprints/Chris Davies)

www.railwaysillustrated.co.uk SULZER POWER 59

FEATURE | Class 44-46

Class 46 46014 makes its way out of Platform 2 at King's Cross with an express for Newcastle on July 10, 1976. (Gavin Morrison)

Looking very smart with its white roof and red bufferbeam, Class 45/1 45114 leaves Sheffield Midland on September 15, 1979 with the 1500 to St Pancras. (John Whiteley)

traction motor blowers and air tanks, were housed in the nose ends.

On top, the roof was made of steel, with the area immediately above the power unit being removable. A boiler tank filling point was also provided at the No 2 end that could be used to take on water from steam-era cranes provided at stations and elsewhere, but these disappeared during the 1960s and the port and associated footsteps in the body side were plated over.

The ten pilot locos were fitted with vacuum train brakes and air brakes on the loco; they never received dual train brakes. The subsequent two varieties were built in the same way, but were later fitted with dual train brakes.

Between the cabs, the engine room was divided into three parts containing the power unit, cooling system, train heating boiler if fitted, and the electrical equipment. The radiator and cooler group, denoted from the outside by the large, square radiator grilles and fan assembly on the roof, was at the No 1 end. The engine and generator compartment was in the middle and the train heating and auxiliary equipment were housed at the No 2 end. The radiator section was also home to the two main fuel tanks. The central section not only had the prime mover and generators, but also the control cubicle, voltage regulator, lubricating oil filter unit, air compressor, vacuum exhauster, main brake cubicle and fuel/water header tanks. The layout of this compartment was not ideal, with restricted access to many components. Not only that, should the air compressor or vacuum exhauster need to be removed, it had to be manhandled out via one of the cabs and could take an entire shift to accomplish. At the No 2 end the steam heat boiler, if fitted, was either a Stones OK4625 or a Spanner Mk III. The compartment also housed the resistance frame, toilet and flush tank, and the boiler water and boiler water treatment tanks.

Class 44-46 | **FEATURE**

Class 45/0 45065 makes an easterly departure from Newcastle on September 14, 1975. However, it will not then head north towards Scotland, but as the 1V52 headcode suggests it will turn south across the High Level Bridge before heading for the South West. (John Whiteley)

Class 45/1 45105 has just departed from Rotherham Masborough with the 0935 Carlisle to Nottingham service on April 21, 1979. The line to the right heads into Booths scrapyard. (John Whiteley)

Electrics

Apart from the style of headcode used, the principle difference between the Class 44/45s and the Class 46 was the type of electrical equipment. For the original ten pilot scheme locos and the next 127 production examples, Crompton Parkinson was the contractor, but for the remaining locos, D138-193 (Class 46), it was Brush.

The Crompton Parkinson main and auxiliary generator unit was on a bed that extended from the engine crankcase. Because engine room space was so tight the auxiliary generator was recessed into the field of the main generator. Driving the wheels were six axle-hung, nose-suspended traction motors, which varied according to the class of loco (see table). The traction motors were all connected in permanent parallel, and the main generator used five stages of field diversion, which was controlled by the load regulator.

The primary control equipment for all variants was by Allen West Ltd and was housed in an electrical cubicle near the combined generator group. All engine starting, field diversion and traction motor switching was controlled by cam-operated contactors.

Initially the batteries powered the air compressor to provide a 40psi air supply to turn the engine over, as well as powering the combined pump set. This soon ran the batteries down, so most locos were fitted with an electromagnetic starting system, with power for control and auxiliary circuits being taken at 220V from the batteries, reduced to 110V by a rotary converter set.

To allow some Peaks to haul the latest air-conditioned stock, 50 were selected to receive an ETH generator between 1973 and 1975. Modification took place at Derby Works during heavy general overhauls and each was fitted with a Brush BL 100-30 Mk III ETH generator, coupled to the existing main/auxiliary generator group. Control equipment was installed in the space

www.railwaysillustrated.co.uk SULZER POWER 61

FEATURE | Class 44-46

A winter scene greets Class 45/0 45004 as it passes Kettlesbeck Bridge with the Heysham to Haverton Hill tanks on December 12, 1981.
(John Whiteley)

Class 44-46 | **FEATURE**

www.railwaysillustrated.co.uk

SULZER POWER 63

FEATURE | Class 44-46

The Midland Main Line will always be associated with the Peaks, particularly the Class 45s. To illustrate the point 45144 has just left Wellingborough with the 1012 Sheffield to St Pancras on April 16, 1982.
(John Whiteley)

Class 46 D143 (46006) makes a powerful sight as it departs from Dawlish with a westbound service on September 1, 1972.
(Gavin Morrison)

vacated by the removal of the steam heat boiler. Interestingly, the water tanks were kept, but were filled with steel ballast weights and not converted into additional fuel tanks. The locos were reclassified as 45/1, with the steam heat version remaining 45/0. Due to the modifications taking place during overhauls, the locos were not renumbered under TOPS in numerical sequence, as had happened with all other classes, but as they fell due they were either renumbered as a 45/0 or 45/1 depending on the heating type retained or fitted. At the time this caused a great deal

Class 44-46 | FEATURE

of confusion among young trainspotters!

The Blue Star multiple working system was included in all Peaks when built, but was rarely used and was removed during works overhauls during the 1960s.

Prime mover

The power unit selected for the first ten locos, the Sulzer 12LDA28-A, was built at the company's Winterthur Works in Switzerland and they were dispatched to the UK as fully finished and tested units. The four-stroke, pressure-charged, direct injection unit was rated at 2,300bhp (1,715kW) at 750rpm and was of a twin-bank design – effectively two in-line six units joined together to drive a common output flange through a straight step-up gear. The subsequent 183 locos were all fitted with the more powerful 12LDA28-B variant, which was inter-cooled and rated at 2,500bhp (1,864kW). They were not built in Switzerland, but instead were manufactured under licence by Vickers Armstrong at Barrow-in-Furness; the order included seven spares.

To test the inter-cooler concept, the 12LDA28-A engine from D2 (44002) was modified with a charge air inter-cooler to increase power to 2,500hp.

Far left: Fresh out of Derby Works following an overhaul and conversion to a Class 45/1, 45111 *Grenadier Guardsman* looks immaculate in August 1973. (Rail Photoprints/Dave Cobbe Collection)

Below: 45122 has just passed Neville Hill Depot as it makes its way into Leeds with the 1322 Newcastle to Liverpool service on September 17, 1983. (John Whiteley)

It caused considerable wear to some engine components and after the trials it reverted to its original specification, but it served as a prototype for the B version of the engine fitted to the production locos. Another loco tested with engine trials was D57 (45042), whose power unit was modified to 12LDA28-C specification by fitting an updated inter-cooler as well as new pistons and connecting rods. The unit produced 2,750hp (2,051kW) and was the prototype for the prime mover to be fitted to the Brush Type 4 (Class 47). It ran in this form between May 1962 and February 1964, before its engine was de-modified to B specification. ➜

SULZER POWER 65

FEATURE | Class 44-46

Liveries

1	Still SYP Oct 1970; FYE by May 1971; Blue November 1971
3	FYE after August 1972; Rail Blue June 1973
6	FYE by July 26, 1970; Rail Blue September 1973
10	FYE after May 1972; Rail Blue December 1972
25	Photographed FYE February 15, 1969; ex-works Rail Blue August 30, 1969
26	Recorded at Newport January 2, 1969 FYE; Rail Blue April 1969
138	FYE applied February 1971; Rail Blue November 1971
154	FYE applied March 1971; Rail Blue February 1972.
155	FYE applied February 1971; Rail Blue September 9, 1971.
159	FYE applied between February 1, 1971 and April 10, 1971; Rail Blue March 1972
166	FYE by July 1969; Rail Blue October 1970
188	FYE by August 1969; Rail Blue July 1970
193	FYE by January 1970; Rail Blue December 1970

The finishing touches are applied to the departmental livery of 97403 (ex-46035) at Toton on April 17, 1985. (Gavin Morrison)

Liveries

Like many BR diesels the Peaks only wore two liveries – BR green and BR blue. The first locos were all-over green, but the requirement for better visibility saw small yellow warning panels applied. However, unlike most other classes, very few Peaks had full yellow ends and green livery (see above).

BR blue quickly became the universal colour and Class 46 D184 was the first to receive it in 1966, with Class 44 6 *Whernside* the last to go blue in September 1973. Towards the end of their careers some locos received celebrity repaints, such as D4 *Great Gable* into green in 1980, while some Class 45s had white stripes applied to replicate those worn by the green locos.

Service

As the first production locos (later Class 45) began to roll off the assembly lines at Derby and Crewe works, most were sent to the Midland Region. Allocated to Derby, Cricklewood and Toton, they were used to phase steam out on the route to St Pancras. In early 1960, D11 and D14 were loaned to Neville Hill on the North Eastern Region for crew training to allow the locos to take over the through St Pancras to Glasgow services that ran via the Settle to Carlisle line.

St Pancras Station was not at its best during the 1970s and always had a grubby feel about it – a far cry from today's modern international facility. Peaks ruled the roost 40 years ago as 45115 departs with the 1801 for Sheffield on May 6, 1978. (Gavin Morrison)

The following year D13 was dispatched to Sheffield Darnall to perform tests with up to 14 coaches between Doncaster and Peterborough. In March 1961, D11-D16 were transferred to Leeds Holbeck for use on the 'Thames-Clyde' and 'Waverley' expresses, and more followed during the summer to take up the remaining Leeds to Glasgow trains.

A Peak (D93) was loaned to the Western Region's Bristol Bath Road Depot in the summer of 1961 to train crews on the type in preparation for cross-country services from Bristol to the North East. However, it wasn't until the 1970s, as the diesel hydraulics were phased out, that the WR actually got a proper allocation.

The Brush-equipped variant began to enter service in 1961 and the fleet was allocated to Derby (D138-165) and Gateshead (D166-193). Initially the Derby-based examples were put to work on the same LMR duties as the earlier production batch, while the Gateshead locos powered the aforementioned cross-country services as well as trains to Liverpool and along the length of the East Coast Main Line between Edinburgh and King's Cross. The Derby Class 46s were all transferred to Laira and Bristol Bath Road in 1971 and began to dominate services between the South West and the North East until they were displaced by HSTs, notably during the early 1980s.

Class 44-46 | FEATURE

Peaks were not often seen on freightliners, but on May 31, 1977 45047 passes Chaloners Whin Jn south of York with a single set of five container flats. (Gavin Morrison)

Although Tinsley applied several livery embellishments to its Peaks during their final years, Toton was not as active, although it did add some white highlights to 45013, as seen on August 4, 1986. (Gavin Morrison)

The only Class 46 to carry a name was 46026 *Leicestershire and Derbyshire Yeomanry* – photographed at Holbeck Depot on October 18, 1979. (Gavin Morrison)

Double heading by Peaks was not common, but on August 2, 1975 45132 leads 45030 and just six coaches forming the Saturdays only 0821 Leeds to Poole service past Oakenshaw North Signal Box. This was most likely a positioning move for the 45/1. (Gavin Morrison)

www.railwaysillustrated.co.uk SULZER POWER 67

FEATURE | Class 44-46

Class 45/0 45069 nears Dawlish Warren with the 0900 Paignton to Birmingham service on July 30, 1983.
(John Whiteley)

Class 44-46 | FEATURE

BR Type 4 (Class 44-46) - Technical data

Class	44	45/0 and 45/1	46
Builder:	BR Derby	BR Derby, BR Crewe	BR Derby
Introduced:	1959-60	1960-62	1961-63
Number Series:	D1-D10	D11-D137	D138-D193
TOPS number series:	44001-44009	45001-077, 45101-150	46001-056
Former class codes:	D23/1, later 23/1	D25/1 (25/1) D25/1 (25/1)	25/1A
Number Built:	10	127	193
Wheel Arrangement:	1Co-Co1	1Co-Co1	1Co-Co1
Route Availability:	7	7 (45/1 6)	6
Multiple working:	Blue Star	Blue Star (45/0)	-
Engine:	Sulzer 12LDA28A	Sulzer 12LDA28B	Sulzer 12LDA28B
Horsepower:	2,300	2,500	2,500
Main Generator:	Crompton CG426A1	Crompton CG426A1	Brush TG160-60
Aux Generator:	Crompton CAG252A1	CAG252A1	Brush TG69-28
Traction Motors:	Crompton C171B1	C172A1	TM73-68
Train Heat (steam)	Stones OK 4625	Stones OK 4625 ETH (45/1)	Stones OK 4625 Spanner Mk 111
Brakes (Locomotive):	Air	Air	Air
Brakes (Train):	Vacuum	Vacuum/Air	Vacuum/Air
Brake Force:	63 tonnes	63 tonnes	63 tonnes
Maximum Tractive Effort:	70,000lbs	55,000lbs	55,000lbs
Power at rail:	1,800hp	2,000hp	1,960hp
Length:	67ft 11in	67ft 11in	67ft 11in
Width:	8ft 10 1/2in	8ft 10 1/2in	8ft 10 1/2in
Height:	12ft 10 1/4in	12ft 10 1/4in	12ft 10 1/4in
Weight:	138 tonnes (later 133)	138 tonnes (later 135)	138 tonnes
Wheel Diameter:	3ft 9in (pony 3ft)	3ft 9in (pony 3ft)	3ft 9in (pony 3ft)
Max Speed:	90mph	90mph	90mph
Fuel Tank:	840 gallons	840 gallons	790 gallons
Boiler water capacity:	1,340gallons	1,040 gallons	1,040 gallons

Run down

The Class 44s began to disappear during the 1970s, and the first Class 45s were withdrawn in 1981; this was mainly due to an over-supply of locomotives, due to the arrival of more HSTs and a reduction in freight demand. The last example was taken out of service in 1989. The Class 46s did even worse, with the first going in 1977 and the last in 1984.

The 1980s saw several projects and trials take place, some of which utilised surplus Peaks. During the decade, BR was researching ways to improve adhesion. A Class 46 (46035) was chosen for the dynamic testing of various wheel/rail interface projects and in 1985 it was modified at Toton for this purpose. This involved amending the centre-powered wheelset at the No 1 end with a separately excited traction motor, and installing equipment to allow the wheelset to rotate independently, with the power regulated by Laboratory Coach 10, to which the Peak was coupled. The loco was christened *Ixion* and is now preserved at Peak Rail.

A rather more spectacular end befell 46009 (46023 was the backup), which was used to demonstrate the strength and integrity of 48-tonne nuclear flasks on July 17, 1984 in an event organised by the Central Electricity Generating Board. The British Rail Board approved the use of the Old Dalby Test Track for the exercise. The flask was position on a dead end piece of track at one end of the line and the Class 46, along with three redundant Mk 1 coaches, was run up to 100mph. To achieve this, special equipment was needed, including an external brake pipe valve. This was set to 'open' as the loco was started and the power controller was opened to full power and the brake handle set to the release position. The driver and engineering staff vacated the cab and, once clear, the brake pipe valve was closed. When the air pressure built up, the Control Circuit Governor closed and power was applied to the traction motors. The AWS and Drivers Safety Device were also isolated. Once in motion there was no way to stop the train – except when it hit the flask. The demonstration was deemed a complete success as the flask was completely intact, but the loco was destroyed and the Mk 1s were written off too. Among the 400 invited guests who witnessed the staged crash were MPs, peers, councillors, trade unionists and industrialists, as well as railwaymen and members of the press. It was also beamed live on national television.

The British Railways-designed Peaks were popular with crews and enthusiasts; they proved to be pretty reliable and their weight, although a disadvantage in many ways, provided good adhesion qualities. They ranged across the whole BR network, although visits to the Southern Region, West and North Wales and anywhere north of Edinburgh and Glasgow in Scotland were quite rare. The Sulzer power plant, which was developed as the 'C' variant for the later standard BR Type 4 (Class 47), was particularly robust. Fortunately several have survived into preservation and serve as a reminder of one of the most successful medium to high powered locos of the 1955 modernisation plan. **5**

SULZER POWER 69

FEATURE | HS4000 Kestrel

ABOVE: Shortly after its official handover to the BRB at Marylebone Station on January 29, 1968, HS4000 *Kestrel* took a rake of Mk 1 stock to Princes Risborough and back, running as the 1Z18 and 1Z19. The formation stands at Princes Risborough. (Colin J Marsden)

The evolving motorway network coupled with a growing internal airline market in the 1960s made British Railways re-evaluate its need for higher powered Type 5 locomotives for both passenger and freight traffic. In early 1965 it expressed an interest in a loco of up to 5000hp.

Meanwhile, in the first half of the 1960s, Brush Electrical Equipment Ltd (Brush) was developing the use of both electronics and AC power generation for locos, which helped in the development of a single-engine traction unit of much higher power than was hitherto possible. Studies had shown that this arrangement was more economical in terms of initial capital cost, maintenance and fuel consumption than either a multi-engined loco (such as a Deltic) or a master-and-slave combination. A further factor was that Sulzer had developed an up-rated version of its LVA24 diesel, which passed the UIC rating test at 4,000 metric horsepower (3,946bhp) at 1,100rpm in 16-cylinder form.

During the mid-1960s, the BR Chief Mechanical and Electrical Engineer was considering the production of a 4,000hp diesel to meet anticipated demand for more powerful traction. It seems Brush, with the backing of its parent Hawker Siddeley, felt sufficiently encouraged by the BR CM&EE to produce a prototype 4,000hp loco using the new Sulzer engine and AC power generation. *Kestrel*, the name given to the loco on completion, was under way by 1965.

Design

Construction of the loco, Works Number 711 of 1967, was undertaken at Brush's Falcon Works in Loughborough alongside the final Brush Type 4s, with the Sulzer diesel, one of five built, being assembled

HS4000 Kestrel | **FEATURE**

HS4000 KESTREL
The Great Experiment

In its day, *Kestrel* was the most powerful locomotive to run in the UK but, despite its technical achievements, it never achieved its full potential. David Clough and Ian MacLean examine the reasons why.

in France. The original test engine was scrapped in Oberwinterthur and three others ended up in power stations: two at Schaffhausen in Switzerland and one at Dunkirk in France. A Brush AC traction generator was used and, after being rectified to DC, the power was supplied to six Brush traction motors, a development of those first used in BR Classes 31 and 46. Brush also equipped HS4000, the allocated BR stock number, to test an electronic traction control system. It also used inertial filters as part of the engine room air management arrangements and included a dynamic braking system, all of which paralleled the contemporary features being built into English Electric Class 50.

Brush opted for a Co-Co wheel arrangement on Commonwealth pattern bogies, which the company had used previously in its Type 2 and 4 designs. While the design top speed was 130mph, the maximum service speed was 125mph, with full engine output available between 18mph and 100mph. With the continuous rating speed of 27½mph, the traction characteristic was clearly for mixed traffic duties.

The use of a stressed-skin superstructure mirrored that adopted for the Brush Type 4. Cab front styling was semi-streamlined and incorporated a wrap-around Triplex windscreen, while a striking two-tone bodyside external livery of yellow (upper) and chocolate brown (lower) with grey for the roof was chosen.

The design weight was for a 21-ton axle-load and 126 tons in total, but when HS4000 was weighed on January 20, 1968 at Derby Works, it turned out to be much higher at more than 133 tons.

Nine days later, a handover ceremony was conducted at Marylebone, with the

FEATURE | HS4000 Kestrel

Hawker Siddeley, Brush and BR chairmen in attendance, followed by a demonstration run to Princes Risborough. Prior to these events, the Hawker Siddeley chairman had written to his opposite number at BR, firstly to thank him for help provided by BR's technical staff during the design work, but secondly to request assistance with publicity and trial running. The Hawker Siddeley chairman was hoping that BR would commit to buying a production version of *Kestrel*, but the BR chairman felt unable to oblige. He was willing to assist with publicity to win export orders, but emphasised that the Board was re-evaluating its future traction needs.

After the handover and demonstration run, HS4000 returned to Falcon Works to await the start of its trials. The Eastern Region Civil Engineer would only permit a 75mph top speed because the maximum axle-load was well above the 21-ton limit.

Trials and service

Nothing more was heard of it until it ran light to Crewe on May 6, 1968, when problems with the dynamic brake were noted. The next day it undertook a light engine run to Llandudno, with the same issue once again noted. Test running continued, including a run over Shap with a 20-coach 670-ton train, with the summit cleared at 46mph. This matched the speed a 2,700hp Type 4 would have achieved, but only with 450 tons. On a further run, with a stop on the incline, the train was restarted without wheelslip, but the engine was found to be overheating.

Meanwhile, the BR Chief Civil Engineer had laid down a maximum axle-load of 20 tons for running up to 100mph, which ruled HS4000 out of work on passenger diagrams. BR seemed reluctant to take the prototype for service running but eventually relented under pressure from Brush, which felt it had been developing a traction unit in conjunction with the Railways' CM&EE.

BR proposed the haulage of freight trains, but these would have to involve the crews at just one depot to minimise training. On May 13, 1968, HS4000 travelled to Tinsley, where it was allocated. Out-based at Shirebrook, a Brush Class 47 diagram was assigned to the loco. Two days later running began, comprising

LEFT: *Kestrel* under assembly at Brush's Falcon Works in 1967, with the 4,000hp Sulzer powerplant being lowered into the engine room. (Brush via Ian MacLean)

LEFT: An official Brush publicity image of the loco shortly after it was completed in late 1967. (Brush via Ian MacLean)

HS4000 Kestrel | FEATURE

ABOVE: The loco stands in the RTC yard at Derby in 1968, wired up to a test train. (Colour-Rail)

RIGHT: *Kestrel* passes Greetwell Junction, Lincoln on May 23, 1968 while working the 7J31 1109 Mansfield Colliery Sidings to Whitemoor Yard. (Colin J Marsden collection)

BELOW: In May 1968 HS4000 powered a 670-ton test train between Crewe and Carlisle during a series of high output tests. The highlight was the demonstration of its ability to top Shap at an impressive 46mph with 20 coaches in tow. (Colin J Marsden collection)

of two return trips each weekday between Mansfield and Whitemoor Yard hauling coal trains with a gross loaded weight of between 1,450 to 1,600 tons. The trains were:
- 7J31 1109 Mansfield Colliery Sidings-Whitemoor, arriving at 1420;
- 7P31 1510 return empties;
- 7J07 1940 Mansfield Colliery Sidings-Whitemoor, arriving at 2253;
- 5P07 2345 Whitemoor Down Yard-Thoresby Colliery Jn

Heavier loads were impractical due to the length limits imposed by loops and sidings, while the wagons had a maximum permitted speed of 35mph. This operating regime was not taxing for so powerful a machine and during one measured daily cycle, 19 hours were spent in traffic, but a mere six minutes on full power.

Kestrel was out of service on May 28 due to a leak on the upper surface of the underslung fuel tank. Further disruption to its mileage accumulation occurred during June and July due to industrial action before things returned to normal on July 9. Saturday, July 20 saw it run light to Manchester for high-speed tests at up to 100 mph to Wilmslow the following day, under the supervision of Derby research staff. It returned light to Tinsley, then to Shirebrook on July 22 to resume its coal work.

On August 2 *Kestrel* was sent for display at Ratcliffe Power Station, before returning to Brush for power tests and checks to its dynamic braking system. Back at Shirebrook, it underwent tests, hauling a rake of 52 32-ton hoppers, weighing 2,028 tons, from Mansfield to Lincoln. It was the heaviest train to run on BR hauled by a single loco and *Kestrel* performed admirably, including starting the train on a rising 1 in 150 wet railhead on Broughton bank.

It went to Derby on August 9 for a B-exam before moving to the Railway Technical Centre, where it was noted on August 24. *Kestrel* was next used on circular test trains from Derby via Crewe, Nuneaton and Leicester for three days, then on August 31 it was displayed at the Derby Loco Works Open Day. The circular test runs resumed on September 9 and continued on and off, with a Class 86 occasionally being added to the rear of the formation between Crewe and Nuneaton. The loco returned to Shirebrook on November 22 to resume its mundane coal work.

After a C-exam at Tinsley on March 28, 1969, *Kestrel* briefly worked its regular turn to Whitemoor on March 31 and April 1 before returning to Brush the next day to be fitted with a set of Class 47 bogies to permit limited 100mph running. It remained at Brush until June, then moved to Derby to be weighed again; it was still over the 20-ton axle weight required by BR.

Kestrel returned to its coal diagram, punctuated by an exhibition at Cricklewood Depot Open Day on July 12. On July 30 it was used on a high-speed test run, powering the 1G13 1135 Doncaster to Peterborough, arriving at 1238 with load six, crewed by Shirebrook men with a Doncaster conductor. It returned as the 1330 Peterborough to Doncaster arriving at 1435, after which it went to Tinsley for an E-exam with 3,275 engine hours accumulated. It was back on its regular diagram on August 6 before being displayed at Barrow Hill Open Day on September 14.

SULZER POWER · 73

FEATURE | HS4000 Kestrel

The mighty loco ran light to Finsbury Park on October 6 for driver training, but it was stopped two days later with an earth fault on its alternator and was taken to Stratford DRS to have the component changed. It was back at Finsbury Park on October 14 for use on a test run from King's Cross to Peterborough the next day, which was not without incident as a traction motor flashed over on the return journey. It returned to Stratford to have the motor changed before undertaking another test run to Peterborough and back to King's Cross on October 18, again load six, but with four catering vehicles. After this it ran light to Finsbury Park to be prepared for its debut on a timetabled passenger train.

The auspicious day was October 20, when *Kestrel* powered the 1N06 0755 King's Cross to Newcastle as far as York. What happened next is unclear, but an official Brush photo also shows it leaving London on the 1L29 1620 King's Cross to York that day.

Kestrel spent the rest of the week working the 1N06 and 1A32 1645 return, apart from October 25 when it worked the 1N08 0900 King's Cross to Newcastle and 1A30 1510 return. 1N06 and 1A32 became the loco's regular diagram, with *Kestrel* putting in some spectacular performances, including a 14-minute early arrival at Newcastle with 1N06 on the booked Deltic timings.

Sadly, its exploits on the East Coast Main Line were cut short in November when the Civil Engineer imposed a 75mph limit due to worries about track damage caused by the overweight loco running at high speed. By the end of the month it was back on the Mansfield-Whitemoor circuit.

The 75mph restriction was briefly lifted so it could work the load 12 1A09 0840 York to King's Cross on December 22 for the benefit of an Australian delegation that had expressed an interest in the loco, but sadly it went no further.

Into the 1970s

After the festive season, *Kestrel* underwent a B-exam at Shirebrook on January 2, 1970. However, an engine fault saw it dragged to Tinsley three days later and it remained at its home depot until January 27 when it was transferred to Doncaster Works to have its power unit removed. Meanwhile, the alternator was sent to Brush for repair and the loco finally returned to Shirebrook on February 27. It was put back to use on the Whitemoor coal until Friday March 6. Three days later it moved to Hull to work the 4C70 1935 Hull-Stratford and the return 4H66 0228 Freightliner trains, where at least the imposed 75mph top speed could be exploited. The loco was serviced at Dairycoates and Stratford, but returned to Tinsley each weekend for exams. The first night ended in embarrassment when an electrical fault saw it fail and it was dragged back to Hull.

Kestrel was released from its Freightliner duties to appear at the Crewe Electric Depot Open Day on April 19, 1970 along with Class 47s 1957 and 1961. By the end of the month it was back at Tinsley for intercooler repairs, which kept it out of service for most of May. Its return to service was short-lived before it was side-lined with engine trouble. The decision was taken to send it to Vickers at Barrow for engine overhaul and it left Tinsley hauled by Class 20 8313 on May 29, but only made it as far as Rose Grove where the LMR refused to accept it due to it being overweight, and the pair retreated to Mirfield. With the paperwork sorted out, *Kestrel* was allowed to continue to Barrow the next day. The overhaul was a protracted affair before it eventually returned to Tinsley on September 2. Its brief career with Freightliner over, *Kestrel* once again resumed its less glamorous existence on the Mansfield-Whitemoor coal. It was, however, still in demand for open days and was on display at the Barrow Hill event on September 27.

There was a slight change to its working pattern in January 1971 when it powered the 1650 Thoresby Colliery-Whitemoor and the 2023 return on the 6th and 7th. But on January 11 it was back on its usual

ABOVE: A 75mph speed restriction for *Kestrel* was briefly lifted so it could work the 12 1A09 0840 York to King's Cross on December 22, 1969 for the benefit of an Australian delegation. This rare image shows the train arriving at its destination. (Brush via Ian MacLean)

LEFT: Mounted on its original heavyweight bogies, *Kestrel* stands at Crewe Works in May 1968 during its initial trials on the LMR. (Colour-Rail/M Burnett)

Kestrel's passenger career was rather brief, mainly confined to late 1969. The loco makes light work of the 1N06 0755 King's Cross to Newcastle near Aycliffe on October 23, 1969. (Rail-Online)

Technical data

Number	HS4000
Introduced	1968
Withdrawn	1971
Wheel Arrangement	Co Co
Engine	Sulzer 16LVA24
Cylinders	16
Horsepower	4,000
Main Alternator	Brush BL120-50
Traction Motors	Brush TM73-68
Train Heat (electric)	Brush BL63-38
Brakes (loco)	Air and dynamic
Brakes (train)	Vacuum, air
Maximum Tractive Effort	70,000lb
Continuous Tractive Effort	41,200lb
Length	66ft 6in
Width	8ft 9¾in
Height	13ft 0½in
Weight	133 tons (see note)
Wheel diameter	3ft 7in
Max speed	125mph
Fuel Tank	1,000 gallons
Number Built	1

Note: When complete, Brush quoted a weight of 126 tons without supplies, possibly in order to meet BR's maximum axle-load of 21 tons. This weight appears to be an estimate because HS4000 was weighed by BR and the Board's CM&EE gave the figure as 144 tons. The weight was reduced by fitting Class 47-pattern bogies, but no reliable source for the outcome of the change to 133 tons has been traced.

RIGHT: In August 1968 *Kestrel* was used on Merry-go-Round coal trains on the Mansfield to Lincoln route weighing up to 2,000 tons. These were the heaviest trains to run on the UK network at the time, with the heaviest reaching 2,028 tons. The loco is seen on one of the trial runs on August 16, 1968; the exact location is not known. (Colin J Marsden collection)

HS4000 Kestrel | FEATURE

ABOVE: During its use on East Coast passenger services, Kestrel prepares to depart from York for King's Cross in October 1969. (Colour-Rail)

ABOVE, RIGHT: Brush publicity material. (Brush via Ian MacLean)

turn and continued as such until it was allegedly withdrawn in March 1971. Reports conflict, however, with the magazine of the Locomotive Club of Great Britain stating that *Kestrel* worked 8P89 2030 Mansfield-Whitemoor on April 13 and returned with 8J89 0035 Whitemoor-Allerton to Mansfield and continued on this duty until it worked 8J89 in the early hours of April 16, while the *Railway Magazine* reported that *Kestrel* was moved from Shirebrook to Crewe Works on April 22.

BR traction policy was shifting away from mixed-traffic to traffic-specific designs and, as built, HS4000 wasn't viewed as suitable for either. Even with Class 47 bogies, the maximum axle-load was above the 20-ton limit for running up to 100mph. In producing a mixed-traffic machine, Brush had designed a very sophisticated and cramped loco that was likely to be a maintenance headache and therefore expensive.

The Russian factor

In view of BR's lack of interest, Brush approached a party of Soviet Union engineers visiting Britain in spring 1969, with a view to a sale. Negotiations were very protracted, not least because of resistance from the Soviet locomotive building industry. The loco was taken to Crewe as by this time the rail connection to the Falcon Works, where locomotive production had ceased, had been severed. At Crewe the original bogies had their wheelsets changed to the Russian 1,520mm gauge before *Kestrel* was hauled to Cardiff on a pair of Class 47 bogies by Class 24 5027 on June 7. The next day it was loaded aboard the Soviet ship *KPACHOKAMCK* at Cardiff Docks bound for Leningrad where, upon arrival, it was united with its re-gauged bogies by staff from Leningrad Varshavskoe Depot and made ready for onward movement to Shcherbinka.

Before the sale it was arranged for HS4000 to be exhibited at a major railway exhibition in Leningrad (now St Petersburg) during July 1971. *Kestrel* had been invited to attend because the Russians thought they could secure a better price if it was already in Russia, thus saving Brush the cost of repatriating it. From the British point of view, Brush had accepted the invitation because it was confident of concluding the sale. It initially put a price of £205,820 on the deal; £158,750 for the loco, £25,900 for the electrical equipment, £15,000 for the Sulzer power plant and £7,070 for spares. After months of difficult negotiations, Russia paid £127,000.

After crew training, testing began to

FEATURE | HS4000 Kestrel

investigate *Kestrel*'s operating characteristics and the reliability of its systems and assembly on the October Railway in April 1972 and continued until September. A total of 30 trips were made, totalling 15,304km. Tests with passenger stock showed that *Kestrel* used more fuel than the Soviet TEP60 diesels. Difficulties were also experienced with frequent electrical failures and the loco spent long periods out of traffic awaiting British engineers to fly out to attend the problems.

Further dynamic tests were carried out on the Ozerskaya branch, near the town of Kolomna on the Moscow Railway and on an experimental high-speed section between Belorechenskaya and Maikop that allowed speeds up to 160km/h (100mph). The tests proved that the loco could run safely at high speed and concluded that the cab environment was better than that on the Soviet locos. Traction and thermal tests were conducted at the closed loop at Shcherbinka to evaluate the power unit, cooling system and electronics. The trials included working 1,000-ton service passenger trains and freights weighing up to 2,600 tons.

The Russians were impressed by the 16LVA24 power unit, but not so by the UTK30 turbocharger, which did not perform as well as the Soviet models despite being more sophisticated. Use of Shell Talona 972 lubricating oil had been specified, but Soviet M14VI oils compared favourably. The electrical and cooling systems performed well and the auxiliary generator that powered the radiator fans and traction blower motors particularly impressed.

The Russians felt the purchase of *Kestrel* had been justified in that it had proved to be an advanced loco and had enabled Russian designers and operators to change their perspective and see a new approach. However, in line with the research plan the loco was dismantled in 1973-4 and its main components handed over to the relevant organisations in the Soviet locomotive industry for further study. It had run approximately 19,641 miles in Russia on top of the 136,646 miles accumulated in England. The bodyshell of *Kestrel* was finally broken up in 1993.

Although Brush did not win any orders for a production version of HS4000, its AC power equipment was chosen for BR's Class 56 heavy freight design. **S**

ABOVE: The loco was very popular with open day organisers and it was exhibited at Crewe Electric Depot on April 19, 1970. (Rail Photoprints/Colin Whitfield)

LEFT: The loco's potential unfulfilled in the UK, it was exported to Russia on June 11, 1971 from Cardiff Docks, where it is seen being loaded aboard Soviet ship *KPACHOKAMCK* bound for Leningrad. (Colin J Marsden collection)

BELOW: Hawker Siddeley/Brush HS4000 takes a break from its Freightliner diagram at Hull Dairycoates in April 1970. (Rail Photoprints/Norman Preedy)

MAGAZINE SPECIALS

ESSENTIAL READING FROM KEY PUBLISHING

LIGHT RAIL
A review of the systems past and present in Britain and Ireland.

£7.99 inc FREE P&P*

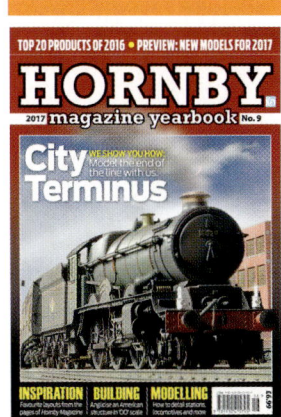

HORNBY MAGAZINE YEARBOOK 9 (BOOKAZINE)
Hornby Magazine creates a 1960s Western Region style city terminus.

£6.99 inc FREE P&P*

HORNBY 2018 CATALOGUE
A perfect showcase for everything our 2018 range has to offer.

£8.99 inc FREE P&P*

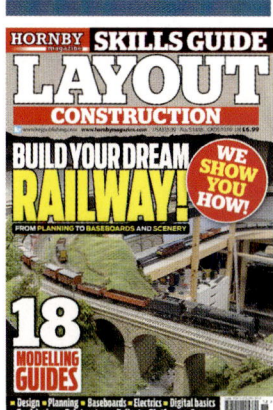

HORNBY MAGAZINE SKILLS GUIDE – LAYOUTS
This 132-page publication will become an essential workbench manual for modellers of all abilities.

£6.99 inc FREE P&P*

HORNBY MAGAZINE GREAT LAYOUTS 2
Featuring 26 favourites from the pages of Hornby Magazine, and scales from 'N' to Gauge 3.

£6.99 inc FREE P&P*

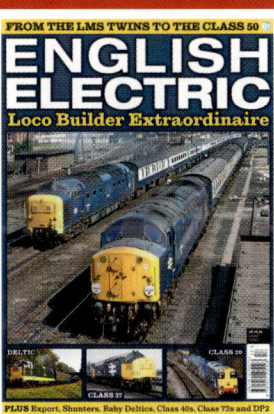

ENGLISH ELECTRIC
This 100-page special publication celebrates the rich history, diversity and product lines of English Electric.

£6.99 inc FREE P&P*

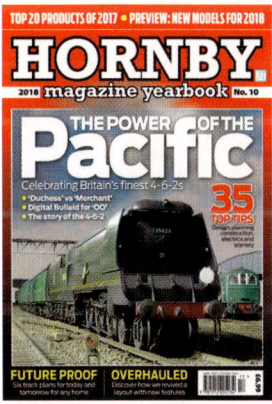

HORNBY MAGAZINE YEARBOOK 10 (BOOKAZINE)
Hornby Magazine is at the forefront of model railway publishing, bringing you informed features and the very latest products.

£6.99 inc FREE P&P*

BR STEAM
The Southern was the final region on British Railways to operate steam-hauled express from a London terminus.

£6.99 inc FREE P&P*

MAGAZINE SPECIALS
ESSENTIAL reading from the teams behind your **FAVOURITE** magazines

HOW TO ORDER

VISIT  OR  **PHONE**
www.keypublishing.com/shop   UK: 01780 480404
ROW: (+44)1780 480404

*Prices correct at time of going to press. Free 2nd class P&P on all UK & BFPO orders. Overseas charges apply. Postage charges vary depending on total order value.

FREE Aviation Specials App
Simply download to purchase digital versions of your favourite aviation specials in one handy place! Once you have the app, you will be able to download new, out of print or archive specials for less than the cover price!

IN APP ISSUES **£3.99**

380/18

FEATURE | Preserved Sulzers

PRESERVED SULZERS

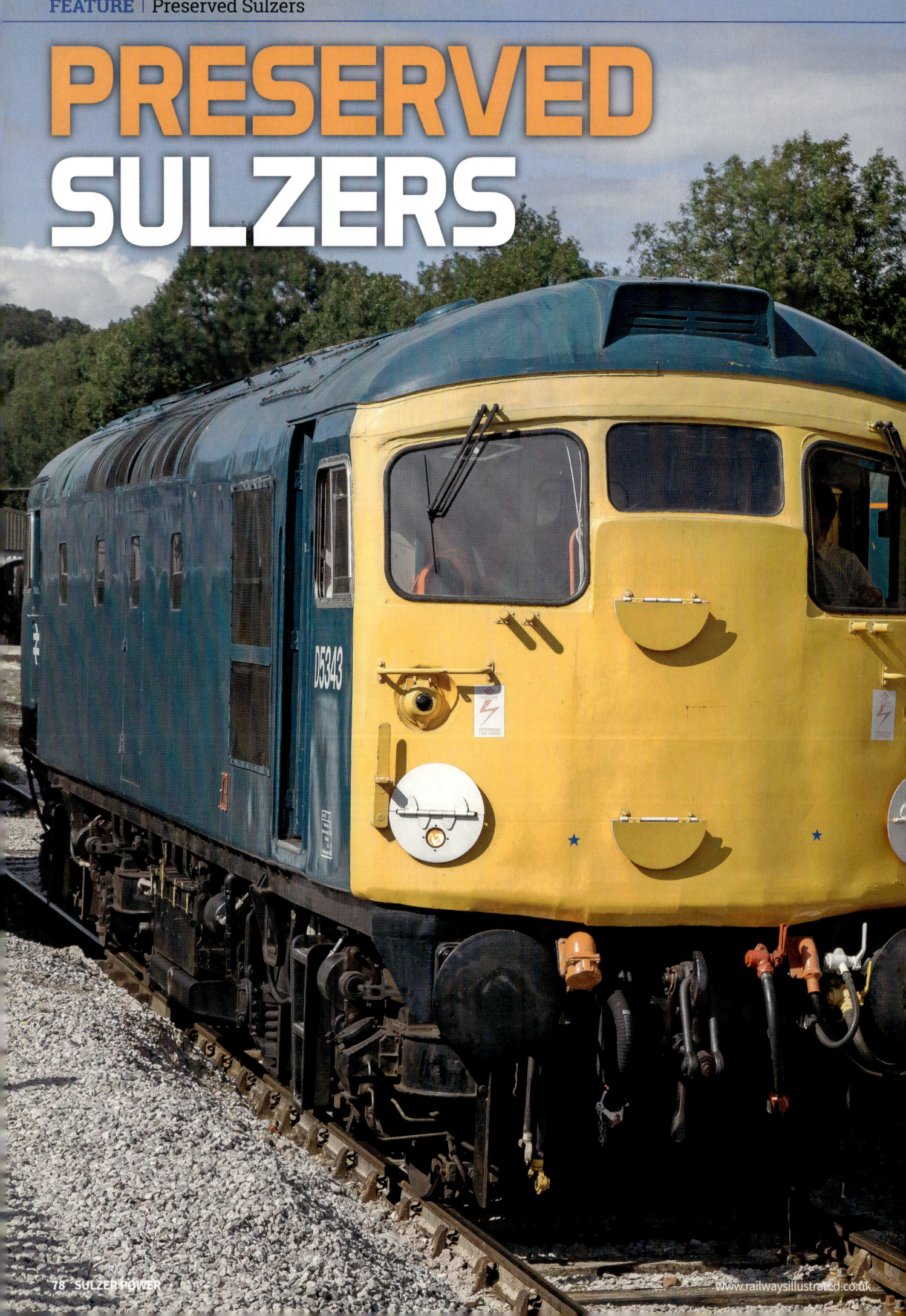

Preserved Sulzers | **FEATURE**

With so many Sulzer-powered locomotives built for British Railways, it is perhaps not surprising that a considerable number have survived into preservation. It is regrettable that the prototype D0260 *Lion* was not saved, given that it was effectively the predecessor of the numerous Class 47, or that HS4000 *Kestrel*, which was exported to Russia, wasn't returned due to its historical significance. However, every other main line type is represented in the heritage sector, with plenty to be seen throughout the year providing valiant service on lines across the UK. Here is a selection of Sulzers to represent the fortunate survivors. **S**

Class 26 D5343 runs around its train and passes 33103 at Wirksworth on the Ecclesbourne Valley Railway prior to working the 1605 to Duffield on August 12, 2017. The 26 usual resides at the Gloucester Warwickshire Railway.
(Richard Hargreaves)

SULZER POWER 79

FEATURE | Preserved Sulzers

Immaculate Class 47 1566 skirts round the curve high above the River Dee on the approach to Berwyn with the 1400 Corwen to Llangollen service on April 13, 2018 during the Llangollen Railway's 'Western Changeover' Gala. (Graham Nuttall)

One of two original pilot scheme survivors is Class 44 D4 *Great Gable*. It was one of the attractions at the Derby Etches Park Depot open day in September 2014. (Wikimedia Commons/Harry Mitchell)

Class 25/3 D7628 at Grosmont, North Yorkshire Moors Railway on October 2, 2017. The loco is main line certified so that it can work the NYMR's services to Whitby. (Mark Nicholls)

One of only three surviving Class 46s, D182 was among the exhibits at the Great Western Railway open day at Bristol St Philips March Depot on May 2, 2016. (Mark Nicholls)

Preserved Sulzers | **FEATURE**

Swanage-based Class 33/0 D6515 *Lt Jenny Lewis RN* arrives back at Weymouth's Platform 2 while working the 5Z42 1652 Yeovil Jn to Swanage on April 13, 2018. Attached at the rear of the five-coach train is ex-SR U Class 2-6-0 No.31806, out on a main line loaded test run. (Stephen Ginn)

Preserved BR Class 24 Bo-Bo D5054 *Phil Southern*, in BR green livery, takes on water for its train heating boiler at Winchcombe on October 25, 2008, while working a Cheltenham Race Course to Toddington service on the Gloucestershire Warwickshire Railway. The loco is now at the East Lancashire Railway.
(Wikimedia Commons/Hugh Llewelyn)

Class 33s 3303 and D6535 pass Woodthorpe with the 1755 Leicester North to Loughborough non-stop service at the Great Central Railway's Spring Diesel Gala on April 14, 2018. (Paul Biggs)

The second surviving Class 44, D8 *Penyghent*, with 45133 at rear, powers away from Sheringham Golf Course with the 1455 Sheringham to Holt service on June 10, 2017 during the North Norfolk Railway's summer 2017 Diesel Gala.
(Paul Biggs)

www.railwaysillustrated.co.uk | SULZER POWER **81**

FEATURE | Preserved Sulzers

The pioneer Class 47, D1500 *North Eastern* (47401), passes through the Golden Valley (Codnor Park Jn to Swanwick Jn) during the Midland Railway Centre's Diesel Gala, on June 18, 2017. (Steve Donald)

Class 45/0 45060 *Sherwood Forester* passes Ruddington Moor while working the 1615 Ruddington to Loughborough service on July 2, 2017. (Bill Pizer)

An EMRPS photo charter on the Keighley & Worth Valley Railway took place on February 25, 2017 and the subject was the line's Class 25/1 25059. The loco stands at Platform 1 with a mixed freight. (Ian Dixon)

Seven coaches and 5,000 horsepower as Class 45s 45060 *Sherwood Forester* and 45133 double head a train past Burrs on the East Lancashire Railway on July 7, 1998. (Gavin Morrison)

Railways Illustrated

NEW! 98-PAGE DIGITAL SAMPLE ISSUE - AVAILABLE NOW!

Your favourite magazine is also available digitally.
DOWNLOAD THE APP NOW FOR FREE.

FREE APP
with sample issue
IN APP ISSUES £3.99

SUBSCRIBE & SAVE
Monthly £2.99
6 issues £19.99
12 issues £34.99

SEARCH: Railways Illustrated

Read on your iPhone & iPad Android PC & Mac  kindle fire Blackberry Windows 10

SEARCH MODERN RAILWAYS
FREE APP with sample issue
IN APP ISSUES £3.99

SEARCH BUSES
FREE APP with sample issue
IN APP ISSUES £3.99

ALSO AVAILABLE FOR DOWNLOAD

FREE Specials App

IN APP ISSUES **£3.99**

Simply download to purchase digital versions of your favourite rail specials in one handy place! Once you have the app, you will be able to download new, out of print or archive specials for less than the cover price!

SEARCH: Aviation Specials

How it Works.
Simply download the Railways Illustrated app and receive your sample issue completely free. Once you have the app, you will be able to download new or back issues (from January 2011 onwards) for less than newsstand price or, alternatively, subscribe to save even more!

Don't forget to register for your Pocketmags account. This will protect your purchase in the event of a damaged or lost device. It will also allow you to view your purchases on multiple platforms.

   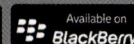 

Available on PC, Mac, Blackberry and Windows 10 from **pocketmags.com**

Requirements for app: registered iTunes account on Apple iPhone, iPad or iPod Touch. Internet connection required for initial download. Published by Key Publishing Ltd. The entire contents of these titles are © copyright 2018. All rights reserved. App prices subject to change. 379/18

FEATURE | Brush Type 4 (Class 47)

The Ubiquitous BRUSH Type 4

Brush Type 4 (Class 47) | **FEATURE**

Shortly after it was delivered to Haymarket following conversion to a 47/7, 47707 *Holyrood* passes Dent Head with the 0835 Glasgow to Euston diverted via the Settle to Carlisle line on May 13, 1979. (John Whiteley)

The Class 47 came about due to complaints regarding the power-to-weight ratios of the early Type 4 diesels designed for British Railways that struggled to equal, let alone exceed, the best performances of Class 8 steam locomotives on passenger trains. The Eastern Region in particular argued in 1959 that something better than the 1Co-Co1 English Electric Type 4s was needed to achieve a 75mph average speed on London services.

Background

With this in mind all three of the principal locomotive suppliers for British Railways were working on new designs. Brush, part of the Hawker-Siddeley Group, was working on *Falcon*, powered by two Bristol-Siddeley Maybach MD655 engines rated at 1,440hp at 1,500rpm. The Birmingham Railway Carriage and Wagon Company project was *Lion*, using the further uprated Sulzer 12LDA28C power unit delivering 2,750hp at 800rpm. The English Electric prototype was DP2, featuring the latest version of the company's 16CSVT engine rated at 2700 hp. These prototypes entered service in September 1961, April 1962 and February 1962 respectively.

Before there was chance to evaluate these prototypes British Railways, which had stated its dislike for twin high-speed engines, seized the opportunity offered

Ian McLean charts the history of the Brush Type 4 (Class 47), the most numerous large diesel ordered by British Railways.

The first Brush Type 4, D1500, emerged from the Loughborough works in early September 1962, and was trialled with a load of 15 bogies between Syston and Cheadle Heath

SULZER POWER 85

FEATURE | Brush Type 4 (Class 47)

by the 2,750hp Sulzer power unit to accelerate the process of dieselisation. In late 1960 it formulated proposals for a Co-Co weighing no more than 114 tons using the engine.

Of the three companies only Brush was able, or willing, to comply with British Railways' wishes. On July 11, 1960 it tendered for the supply of locos based on the existing order of 40 at Loughborough for the electrical equipment for BR 1Co-Co1 (later Class 46) being built at Derby. Twenty units were then cancelled and a new order was placed on February 28, 1961 for a build of 20, numbered D1500-1519.

Even before D1500 had been delivered orders had been made for up to D1706, with locos to be built at both Loughborough and Crewe as the network tried to purge itself of steam. An order for 30 examples (D1520-1549) was placed with Brush in January 1962, along with 33 from Crewe (D1550-1582). More followed in the summer, with Brush awarded two deals for a total of 100 units (D1682-1706 and D1707-1781). At the same time a further 99 (D1583-1681) were commissioned from Crewe. In May 1963 Brush gained another contract for 60 (D1782-1841), with 20 more (D1842-1861) from Crewe. Final orders for 150 locos were placed in March 1964, with Brush building 100 (D1862-1962) and Crewe the remaining 50 (D1962-1999 and D1100-1111).

The Brush Type 4

The first Brush Type 4, D1500, emerged from the Loughborough works in early September 1962, and was trialled with a load of 15 bogies between Syston and Cheadle Heath. In mid-September, D1500 arrived at Cricklewood for a British Transport Commission inspection before being delivered to Finsbury Park Depot, where it was officially allocated on the 28th. It worked its first passenger train on October 8 although it got off to an ignominious start when it was piloted from Grantham by B1 steam loco 61389 due to boiler trouble on the 0810 Kings Cross-Hull to Doncaster. With the problem fixed it returned to London on the 1245 Hull-Kings Cross from Doncaster.

With very little scope to use the electric train heating equipment at the time, the retrograde decision was made to abandon the 800volt train heat generator after the first 20 locos. In order to provide a load for the train heat generator and prevent it from glazing over when trains were steam heated, the compressor, exhausters and radiator fans were all 800volt machines,

Several Type 4 bodyshells under construction at the Brush Falcon Works in Loughborough in the early 1960s. (Colin Marsden Collection)

Brush Type 4 (Class 47) | FEATURE

which the generator supplied. On subsequent locos the electrical machines were 110volt devices, apart from the radiator fan that ran off a high pressure oil system. Another major change was that the new batch had Davies & Metcalfe braking equipment as opposed to Westinghouse on the first 20. Other amendments during production included alterations to the axle design, swapping the wiring of the traction motors from series-parallel to all-parallel, (which necessitated changes to the main generator), the fitting of air brakes for use on Freightliner and Merry-Go-Round (MGR) coal trains, (requiring the fitting of an extra compressor and alterations to the cooling system to accommodate the extra compressor), and changes to the boiler room to enable any of the three types of boiler to be fitted without the need for structural alterations. Slow speed control was also fitted to certain locos for MGR use.

By the end of 1962 it was announced that a batch of 20 of the Hawker-Siddeley Type 4s were to be built for the Western Region. The gradual uprating of the Sulzer 12LDA28 power unit through its A to C forms, coupled with advances in loco design meant that the original power/weight advantages held by the diesel-hydraulics had been cancelled out. Moreover, prices of Type 4 diesel-electrics and their component diesel and electric traction equipment had tended to fall, while the opposite had been the case in diesel hydraulics.

The delivery of the first 20 examples to Finsbury Park allowed for further

D1764 shortly after arrival at Bradford Exchange with the down Yorkshire Pullman in March 1967. (John Whiteley)

In standard BR blue, ETH-fitted 47/4 47437 calls at Rhyl with a Euston to Holyhead service on August 1, 1981. (Adrian Paul)

Not even four months old, D1712 leaves Bristol Temple Meads with an ECS and vans combination on May 16, 1964. The loco had just been reallocated to Bristol Bath Road from Wolverhampton Oxley. (John Whiteley)

FEATURE | Brush Type 4 (Class 47)

Brush Type 4 D1633 stands between duties at the old Saltley Depot in April 1969. For many the BR green livery with full yellow ends suited the design admirably. (Rail Photoprints/Mike Jefferies)

acceleration of Great Northern services in the summer 1963 timetable. This was based on the elimination of the 2,000hp English Electric Type 4s from rostered Class 1 duties, to allow East Coast expresses to be diagrammed only for Deltic, North Eastern Region BR/Sulzer Type 4s or Hawker-Siddeley Type 4s. The deliveries of the Hawker-Siddeleys would also allow for the first withdrawals of Class A4 Pacifics from King's Cross Depot.

D1520, the first of the 'standard' Type 4s, was delivered to Finsbury Park on June 5, 1963, but it would be January 1968 before D1961, the 512th and final member of the fleet, arrived from Loughborough. The length of the delivery span meant that the final two were fitted with Electric Train Heat as well as a boiler. Prior to D1961 entering service, two, D1734 and D1671, had been written off by collision damage in 1965, so there were never more than 510 in service at any one time.

The Western Region received its first delivery, to Old Oak Common, in October 1963 when D1682 replaced the D1000s on Paddington-Birmingham-Birkenhead services. Later that year, D1696 was allocated to the London Midland Region in December 1963, but it would be October 1965 before D1968 became the first of the type to be permanently allocated to the Scottish Region at Haymarket. The only region to miss out was the Southern, but this was temporarily corrected in December 1966/January 1967 when D1921-6 were transferred to Eastleigh to oust steam from the Waterloo to Weymouth route prior to the electrification to Bournemouth. They returned to the Western Region in the latter half of 1968.

Eighty-one Brush Type 4s were built without any train heating equipment and were designated for freight use. The batch later became 47/3s under TOPS and was numbered D1782-1836 and D1875-1900, with the first entering traffic in November 1964. They were allocated to Tinsley (25 locos) and Toton (30), with the final 26 split between Immingham and Tinsley.

Class 48

D1702-6 were delivered out of sequence from Loughborough due to being fitted with 12LVA24 engines rated at 2,650hp. All five initially went to Tinsley, with D1703 leading the way in September 1965. Due to their non-standard nature they were used on freight trains working off Shirebrook, returning to Tinsley for major exams.

A change to their pattern occurred in October 1967 when D1702 and 1704 were noted as regularly working the 1N09 King's Cross to Leeds and 1E85 return. D1705 was noted on the turn for the first time two months later. On January 6, 1967 D1702 was noted on the 1A31 1200 Edinburgh-King's Cross in place of the booked Deltic.

By the summer of 1968, D1702 was dumped at Crewe Works awaiting a decision on its future. This was resolved when 1908 was written off in a collision at Monmore Green on April 8, 1969 and 1702 was re-engined to become a standard Class 47. It was also rewired as series-parallel, a move that would see it eventually outlive all its parallel sisters. In the meantime, 1703 was transferred to Norwich in April 1969, with 1704-6 following in June, for use on Liverpool Street expresses. They gained a reputation for poor reliability and they were gone from the Great Eastern by mid-November. By December 14 all five were in Crewe Works for conversion to standard Class 47s.

Air brakes

Train air brakes were fitted from D1758 onwards for Loughborough-built locos and from D1631 on Crewe-built ones. Modifications during construction saw

Thought to be the first Brush Type 4 to visit Leeds for crew training, 'Generator' D1505 stands at Neville Hill Depot on March 24, 1963. (Gavin Morrison)

Brush Type 4 (Class 47) | FEATURE

Technical data	
BRUSH TYPE 4 (CLASS 47/4)	
Builder	Brush Loughborough/BR Crewe
Introduced	1962-1987
Number Series	47401-47665, 47971-47976
Number Built/converted	263
Wheel Arrangement	Co-Co
Route Availability	6
Engine	Sulzer 12LDA28C
Horsepower	2,580
Main Generator	Brush TG160-60 Mk2, Mk 4 or TM172-50 Mk 1
Traction Motors	Brush TG69-20 or TG69-28 Mk 2
Train Heat	ETH*
Brakes (Locomotive)	Air
Brakes (Train)	Air/Vacuum
Brake Force	60 tons
Maximum Tractive Effort	60,000lbs
Length	63ft 6in
Width	9ft 2in
Weight	117tons
Wheel Diameter (driven)	3ft 9in
Max Speed	95mph
Fuel Tank	720-1,295 gallons

*Some dual heat with a steam boiler.

Technical data	
BRUSH TYPE 4 (CLASS 47/0)	
Builder	Brush Loughborough/BR Crewe
Introduced	1962-1965
Number Series	D1521-D1998
Number Built	50
Wheel Arrangement	Co-Co
Route Availability	6
Engine	Sulzer 12LDA28C
Horsepower	2,580
Main Generator	Brush TG160-60 Mk2, Mk 4 or TM172-50 Mk 1
Traction Motors	Brush TG69-20 or TG69-28 Mk 2
Train Heat	Steam
Brakes (Locomotive)	Air
Brakes (Train)	Air/Vacuum
Brake Force	60 tons
Maximum Tractive Effort	60,000lbs
Length	63ft 6in
Width	9ft 2in
Weight	117tons
Wheel Diameter (driven)	3ft 9in
Max Speed	95mph
Fuel Tank	720-1,221 gallons

Brush Type 4 1712 again, this time in BR blue but with pre-TOPS number under each cab and the double arrows behind each cab door. It is powering a fully loaded train of car flats down Shap at Greenholme on March 13, 1970. (John Whiteley)

a change in the appearance as the fixed radiator grilles at the No 1 end were replaced with louvres due to the removal of the radiator drain tank because of space constraints. D1807 was the first to emerge as such from Brush.

A programme to fit additional air train brakes to locos built with vacuum brakes commenced at Crewe Works in September 1968, with D1576 the first to be treated. As ever with the Class 47s, it took a long time for the process to be completed and 47108 was the last to be dual-braked in August 1976.

Freightliner and MGR

D1807 and D1823 were used on the 0555 Chaddesden to Brent liner test trains during July 1965 and D1816/23/7/30 on similar trials during August. Liner trials commenced from Shawfield in late October, departing at 1300 as 3X28, with D1860 used on October 20 and D1850 three days later. The first revenue-earning Freightliner trains ran between London and Glasgow on the night of November 15, 1965 with D1971 working the 2017 up service. The Type 4s worked such trains for more than 40 years, with 47830 the last to be used on a 'box' train when it powered the 4M93 1758 Southampton Maritime to Garston from Basford Hall in the early hours of December 28, 2007.

D1880 was used on a 4Z10 special from New England to West Burton Power Station hauling 30 loaded 26-ton coal hoppers on October 17, 1966. Starting tests were carried out between Corby Glen and Stoke and between Carlton and Duckmanton. The 47s went on to be a regular sight on such trains for the next 20 years, until their eventual replacement by Type 5s allowed for longer, more economic trains.

FEATURE | Brush Type 4 (Class 47)

Brush supplied ten locos to Cuban National Railways in 1965, although they were delivered with Clayton builder's plates. Two of them (second loco is 2509) stand in a poor state after withdrawal at Cardinas on February 9, 1992.
(Gavin Morrison)

Wearing the mainline version of InterCity livery, Eastfield-based 47470 stands on Doncaster Depot on November 21, 1988. The loco had no InterCity decals and was wearing very small numbers.
(Gavin Morrison)

Stratford-based Class 47/0 47164 was turned out in this splendid patriotic livery to celebrate the Queen's Silver Jubilee in 1977. The loco waits to depart from Liverpool Street with 'The Jubilee' service to Norwich on June 8, 1977.
(Rail Photoprints)

De-rating
The class hit the headlines of the Sunday Times for all the wrong reasons in July 1965 due to fatigue fractures of the engine sump, caused by a mixture of uprating the engine speed to 800rpm and poor weld quality. British Railways was aware of the problem before the press got hold of it and D1773 had already been de-rated to 2,580hp at 750rpm and re-allocated to the RTC at Derby for evaluation. It returned to Vickers of Barrow in February 1966 to have its engine removed and examined and with the problem deemed to be cured plans were made for the fleet to be de-rated. D1974 was the last to arrive at Barrow for 'rebalancing' in June 1967, with any remaining untreated locos to be modified at Crewe Works. Examples still rolling off the production line were delivered at 2,750hp and sent to Barrow for de-rating, while others were de-rated during overhaul.

Push-pull and ETH
A proposal to work Paddington to Birmingham services using the push-pull method resulted in D1938 being fitted with Blue Star equipment. Although plans changed, the WR was still interested in the concept and an eight-coach test set was prepared by the ER, and tests were undertaken on the ECML. D1938 finally arrived on the WR at the end of April 1966.

With 210 air-conditioned coaches already on order for the Eastern Region a programme to fit 47s with a generator to supply electric train heat supply commenced in 1971, with the locos in the 11xx series first to be fitted at Crewe Works during general overhaul. The initial plan for 110 locos was due to run until spring 1974. However, it continued for the next 15 years until eventually 263 of the fleet were modified, with the conversion of 47232 to 47665 the last in March 1987.

Livery
D1733 was the first 47 to switch from the attractive two-tone green livery when it was painted blue at Derby Works in June 1964 for use with the promotional XP64

> The class hit the headlines of the Sunday Times for all the wrong reasons in July 1965 due to fatigue fractures of the engine sump

train. D1953-61 were also delivered in the original BR blue livery from November 1966. Green locos with the addition of full yellow fronts started to appear in July 1967. In early 1968, D1532/47 were the first to be painted blue during overhaul at Crewe Works. The process of painting the entire fleet blue was a long one, with 47256 the last to succumb in October 1978.

The next change was the application of Large Logo livery to 47711/712 in March 1981, although it was September 1985 before 47438 and 47503 emerged from overhaul at Crewe in Large Logo, as the livery became the norm for ETH-fitted locos. A month earlier 47050 had been released in Railfreight livery, which should have become standard for no-boiler 47/0s and the 47/3s, but a misunderstanding at Crewe Works saw only locos in the 470xx and 473xx series released in the colours, with others still being painted blue!

ScotRail's manager at the time, Chris Green, saw the opportunity to build a brand image, and the 47/7s started to be painted in the network's livery in 1984 beginning with 47708. This was the catalyst for sectorisation, which, with subsequent privatisation spawned a proliferation of different liveries, including several one-offs.

Modifications
Yellow warning lights above the cab

90 SULZER POWER

www.railwaysillustrated.co.uk

Brush Type 4 (Class 47) | FEATURE

In Railfreight Red Stripe colours, class 47/3 47301 passes Clay Cross with a northbound train of 100t bogie tanks on September 10, 1988. (Gavin Morrison)

roofs were experimentally fitted to 1979 and 1892 (47277 and 47373) in 1971, with trials taking place at Eggborough Power Station. The aim was to increase productivity: the lights would illuminate as a warning to personnel on the track when MGR trains were moving under remote control at ½ mph, which would then alert the crew to take their break as the train unloaded. Meanwhile 47370 and 47379 were fitted with multiple working equipment and the pair were used to give rides at the Immingham Open Day on September 1, 1974.

During the 1972 miners' strike 1900 was noted wired-up at Sheffield Midland station on February 5, earmarked to provide an emergency electric supply. Later in the week it was replaced by 1884.

More famously Stratford's 47155 was loaned to the CEGB for use as a stationary generator set at West Thurrock Power Station in Essex. The loco was lifted from its bogies at Stratford Depot and taken to the power station by haulier Pickfords during the night of January 8, 1976. It was set to run with an output equivalent to that produced for traction at 60mph to excite a 300MW turbo alternator following a serious fault on an auxiliary generator at the power station. Although repairs to the faulty power station equipment had been expected to take several months, 47155 was returned to BR during February and was back in traffic in March.

When the system of displaying train reporting numbers ceased in January 1976, it changed the face of the fleet. The original edict was that the headcode should be wound to '0O00' and the winding handles removed, which was superseded by two white dots on a black background – quickly referred to as the 'domino' headcode.

First to have its headcode plated over with metal in March 1976 was the 47425. The change meant collision-damaged locos could be repaired with a 'flush front' and 47244 was first to be noted as such in June 1977, followed by 47282 two months later. Both of these were rudimentary modifications undertaken at depots. Two years later, Crewe Works followed suit, with 47249 and 47061.

A dozen 47s were converted for push-pull operation to replace the top-and-tail Class 27s on the Edinburgh-Glasgow route in 1979. Such was the success, the locos were modified to run at 100mph in 1984 and four more were converted in 1985. The early withdrawal of 47713 due to fire damage in 1988 saw 47497 converted to 47717 as its replacement. Push-pull operation ceased in May 1990 and the

Still based at Haymarket at the time, 47273 at Healey Mills Depot on April 25, 1984 alongside resident 47373. While based at Knottingley 47373, along with 47277, was fitted with remote control equipment for use when unloading at power stations – signified by the flashing orange light above the cab. (Gavin Morrison)

www.railwaysillustrated.co.uk

SULZER POWER 91

FEATURE | Brush Type 4 (Class 47)

Class 47 Survivors

Number	Original	Built	Date	Status	Main line operator
47004	D1524	Brush	14/6/63	Preserved, non-operational	
47105	D1693	Brush	6/12/63	Preserved, under overhaul	
47117	D1705	Brush	4/11/65	Preserved	
47192	D1842	Crewe	15/5/65	Preserved	
47194	D1844	Crewe	22/5/65	Awaiting disposal	
47205	D1855	Crewe	24/7/65	Preserved	
47237	D1914	Brush	1/11/65	Main line	WCR
47245	D1922	Brush	9/12/65	Main line	WCR
47270	D1971	Crewe	30/10/65	Main line, under repair	WCR
47292	D1994	Crewe	16/4/66	Preserved	
47306	D1787	Brush	26/11/64	Preserved, under overhaul	
47355	D1836	Brush	10/4/65	Awaiting disposal	WCR
47367	D1886	Brush	26/8/65	Preserved	
47368	D1887	Brush	17/8/65	Awaiting disposal	WCR
47375	D1894	Brush	3/12/65	Main line in Hungary	CRS
47376	D1895	Brush	1/9/65	Preserved	
47401	D1500	Brush	6/9/62	Preserved	
47402	D1501	Brush	13/11/62	Preserved	
47417	D1516	Brush	10/4/63	Preserved, under overhaul	
47449	D1566	Crewe	23/3/64	Preserved	
47484	D1662	Crewe	20/2/65	Preserved, awaiting overhaul	
47488	D1713	Brush	28/1/64	Stored	Nemesis
47492	D1760	Brush	8/9/64	Awaiting disposal	WCR
47500	D1943	Brush	27/6/66	Stored	WCR
47501	D1944	Brush	29/7/66	Mainline	LSL
47524	D1107	Crewe	23/12/66	Preserved, under overhaul	
47526	D1109	Crewe	10/1/67	Awaiting disposal	WCR
47579	D1778	Brush	23/10/64	Preserved	
47580	D1762	Brush	1/9/64	Main line	SF47G
47596	D1933	Brush	2/3/66	Preserved	
47635	D1606	Crewe	29/7/64	Preserved, under repair	
47640	D1921	Brush	3/12/65	Non-operational	Nemesis
47643	D1970	Crewe	23/10/65	Preserved	
47701	D1932	Brush	24/2/66	Non-operational	Nemesis
47703	D1960	Brush	11/7/67	Non- operational	HNRC
47712	D1948	Brush	1/8/66	Preserved	
47714	D1955	Brush	29/11/66	Non-operational	HNRC
47715	D1945	Brush	30/6/66	Non-operational	HNRC
47727	D1629	Crewe	17/10/64	Main line, under overhaul	GBRf
47739	D1615	Crewe	29/8/64	Main line	GBRf
47744	D1927	Brush	31/1/66	Stored	Nemesis
47746	D1754	Brush	19/8/64	Main line	WCR
47749	D1660	Crewe	13/2/65	Main line	GBRf
47760	D1617	Crewe	4/9/64	Main line	WCR
47761	D1619	Crewe	12/9/64	Preserved, awaiting disposal	

Number	Original	Built	Date	Status	Main line operator
47765	D1643	Crewe	19/12/64	Preserved	
47768	D1725	Brush	24/3/64	Awaiting disposal	WCR
47769	D1753	Brush	21/7/64	Awaiting overhaul	HNRC
47771	D1946	Brush	6/7/66	Preserved, under overhaul	
47772	D1657	Crewe	1/2/65	Main line	WCR
47773	D1755	Brush	14/8/64	Main line	Vintage
47776	D1776	Brush	22/10/64	Stored	WCR
47785	D1909	Brush	19/1065	Preserved, non-operational	
47786	D1730	Brush	28/4/64	Stored	WCR
47787	D1757	Brush	17/9/64	Stored	WCR
47790	D1973	Crewe	10/11/65	Awaiting overhaul	LSL
47798	D1656	Crewe	1/2/65	Preserved, NRM	
47799	D1654	Crewe	23/1/65	Preserved, non-operational	
47802	D1950	Brush	9/9/66	Main line	WCR
47804	D1965	Crewe	2/10/65	Main line	WCR
47805	D1935	Brush	18/3/66	Main line	LSL
47810	D1924	Brush	20/12/65	Overhaul	LSL
47811	D1719	Brush	25/2/64	Stored	LSL
47812	D1916	Brush	18/11/65	Main line	ROG
47813	D1720	Brush	6/3/64	Mainline	ROG
47815	D1748	Brush	1/7/64	Main line	ROG
47816	D1650	Crewe	9/1/65	Stored	LSL
47818	D1917	Brush	3/12/65	Awaiting overhaul	AFS
47826	D1976	Crewe	24/11/65	Main line	WCR
47828	D1966	Crewe	2/10/65	Preserved	
47830	D1645	Crewe	24/12/64	Main line	Freightliner
47832	D1610	Crewe	13/8/64	Main line	WCR
47840	D1661	Crewe	13/2/65	Preserved	
47841	D1726	Brush	24/3/65	Stored	LSL
47843	D1676	Crewe	16/4/65	Stored	ROG
47847	D1774	Brush	19/10/64	Withdrawn	ROG
47848	D1652	Crewe	16/1/65	Main line	ROG
47851	D1648	Crewe	22/1/65	Main line	WCR
47853	D1733	Brush	12/6/64	Overhaul	HNRC
47854	D1972	Crewe	4/11/65	Repairs	WCR

Eighty Class 47s remain as such in February 2018, ranging from freshly overhauled main line locos, to wrecks that have lain derelict awaiting the cutter's torch for years.

Key – Operators

AFL	Arlington Fleet Services
CRS	Continental Railway Solutions
GBRf	GB Railfreight
HNRC	Harry Needle Railroad Company
LSL	Locomotive Services Limited
ROG	Rail Operations Group
WCR	West Coast Railway Company

A pair of Large Logo-liveried 'Generators' at Holbeck Depot on May 25, 1990. On the left is 47407 and on the right 47413; both were withdrawn in March 1994. (John Whiteley)

Brush Type 4 (Class 47) | **FEATURE**

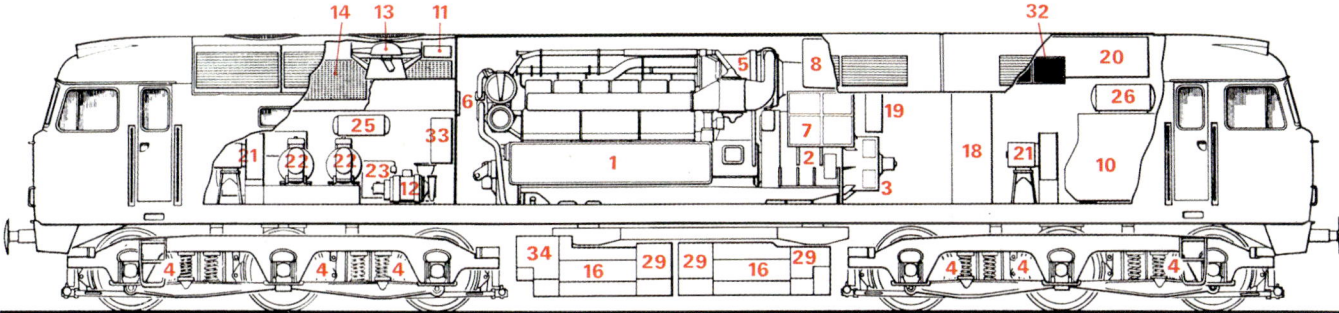

47/7s migrated south.

Although Class 47s had been allocated to Inverness since December 1973 it was seven years before BR finally got round to fitting snowploughs when 47541 and 47546 were modified at Crewe Works in December 1980. The Scottish Region continued to fit locos up until 1987, with 47 003/004/006/017/018/053/117/118/206/210, 47460/461/464/467/469/470/492/550/562/578/593/595/604/617/630/636/641/643 and 644 all completed.

A Sulzer 12LDA28C power unit, with some panels removed, at Crewe Works on June 1, 2003. The round components along the lower side of the engine are Bicera valves, designed to release pressure build up within the crankcase. (Colour-Rail/R Hunter)

Cotswold Rail subsequently fitted 47200 and 47316 and 47245 by West Coast Railways.

Heavy General Overhaul

A programme to restore the 508 remaining Class 47s to as-built condition commenced at Crewe Works in 1976. The work was scheduled to coincide with general overhauls and it was planned to output two per week, with 40 due to undergo the work in 1976, and the full programme taking five years.

The project was designed to enable the 47s to work for another 15 years, into the 1990s, and aimed to reduce costs by making the refurbishment an extension of the 12-yearly general overhaul. To maintain the programme more youthful units would be treated if necessary.

The first candidate was 47293, arriving at Crewe Works on December 5, 1975. About half the fleet had been done by September 1979 with the programme completed in 1982.

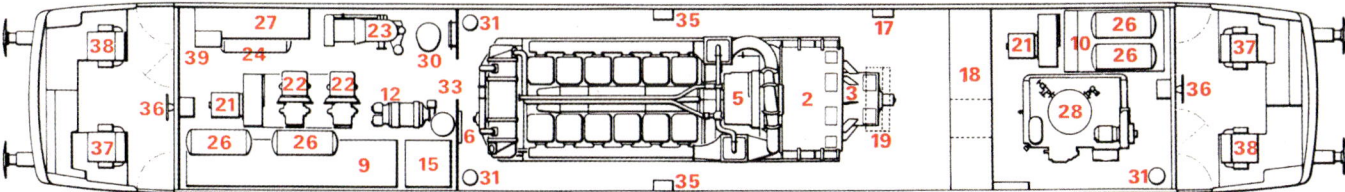

The interior layout of a Class 47: **1** Sulzer 12LDA28 engine, **2** main generator, **3** auxiliary generator, **4** traction motors, **5** pressure charger, **6** engine instrument panel, **7** engine air filter, **8** silencer, **9** No 1 fuel tank, **10** No 2 fuel tank, **11** radiator header tank, **12** combined pump set, **13** radiator fans, **14** radiator panels, **15** main coolant tank, **16** battery boxes, **17** battery isolating switch, **18** main control cubicle, **19** rotary switch and fuse panel, **20** resistance frame, **21** traction motor blowers, **22** exhausters, **23** air compressor, **24** main air reservoir, **25** control air reservoir, **26** auxiliary air reservoirs, **27** brake gear cubicle, **28** steam generator, **29** boiler water tanks, **30** toilet, **31** fire extinguisher, **32** air filter panels, **33** hydrostatic oil tank, **34** measuring and drain tanks, **35** boiler water filler, **36** handbrake wheel, **37** driving seat, **38** secondman's seat, **39** cooker. (Colin Marsden Collection)

FEATURE | Brush Type 4 (Class 47)

The testbed
The events of September 29, 1974 would be far-reaching for 47046 when it was badly damaged in a derailment north of Peterborough. It had been overhauled at Crewe Works only ten months earlier, when it was also fitted with air brakes and renumbered from 1628, but the decision was taken to use it to test the power equipment in the forthcoming Class 56s. However, the whole process was a disaster as the loco was not released to traffic at Tinsley as 47601 until December 1976, by which time the first 56s were already in the country.

In September 1978, 47601 returned to Crewe Works for conversion to 47901 as a testbed for the power unit for the Class 58, and was first based on the Western Region. It arrived in South Wales in June 1980 and was initially used on coal trains, before moving to Bristol, where it was generally out-based at Westbury on stone traffic until it was withdrawn as non-standard in March 1990.

Names
Apart from some Western Region Brush Type 4s in the 1960s, it was several years before any further namings took place. Having got away with embellishing 47163 and 47164 with Union Flags for the Silver Jubilee in 1977, an emboldened Stratford Depot started to give its 47s non-standard grey roofs. They went one step further in April 1978 when 47460 was bestowed with *Great Eastern* nameplates made with car number plate lettering. The BR Board were not impressed and the nameplates were removed 18 days later, but the mould had been broken.

The Board relented in 1979 and 47701 was the first of the class to be named since the original Western Region examples when it emerged from conversion at Crewe Works in January bearing *Saint Andrew* plates. The Western Region then got in the act when 47500 was named *Great Western* on February 27 and the Eastern finally caught up when 47169 became *Great Eastern* on March 7. The London Midland joined the party, naming 47555 *The Commonwealth Spirit* on April 9.

The Jinx Loco
It seems scarcely believable, but 47216 was renumbered 47299 in December 1981 after a clairvoyant predicted the loco would be involved in a fatal collision. It was to no avail as the foresight was proved true in a fatal collision with a DMU at Wrawby Junction, Barnetby on December 9, 1983. During the repairs to 47299 its appearance was further altered by the removal of the cab skirting. This was an attempt to improve the notoriously draughty cabs of the 47s and 47299 was the first of 217 to be modified, with 47815 the last in November 1998.

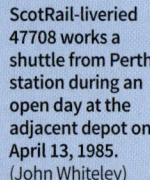
Wearing InterCity livery, 47609 stands outside the depot at Bristol Bath Road. (Mike Goodfield)

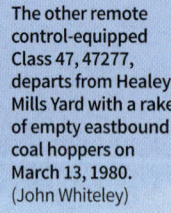
ScotRail-liveried 47708 works a shuttle from Perth station during an open day at the adjacent depot on April 13, 1985. (John Whiteley)

The other remote control-equipped Class 47, 47277, departs from Healey Mills Yard with a rake of empty eastbound coal hoppers on March 13, 1980. (John Whiteley)

94 SULZER POWER

Brush Type 4 (Class 47) | **FEATURE**

Withdrawals

A fatal crash occurred on October 22, 1979 when 47208, hauling the 0935 Glasgow to Aberdeen, ploughed into the rear of the failed 0844 Glasgow to Dundee hauled by 25083 near Invergowrie. The 47s became the first TOPS numbered 47 to be withdrawn.

The first intact 47s were withdrawn in March 1986 when 47405/414/416 were condemned to yield spares for the other 'Generators'. Further inroads to the fleet were made that year as 47111/275/282/464 were also written off due to collision damage, 47403/408/409 as non-standard and 47001 due to body fractures.

The first of the type to be preserved was 47001, which was donated to the Crewe Heritage Centre in 1988. However, it was swapped for 47192 later in the year as the latter was in better mechanical condition and, more significantly, Crewe-built.

Sectorisation

April 1987 saw a big change to how BR was run with the organisation being split into business sectors. A total of 489 47s were 'sectorised', with Freight operators taking the lion's share at 247. InterCity got 85, Provincial 61, Parcels 45, Departmental 41 and Network SouthEast five. Five of the 'Generators' that were slated for early withdrawal were not allocated to a sector.

Upon privatisation the Charter Unit was sold to record producer and songwriter Pete Waterman in May 1994, with six Class 47s (47701/3/5/9/10/12) being part of the deal. Rail Express Systems (Res) was sold to Wisconsin Central in December 1995, including 110 operational 47s and another eight stored examples. Wisconsin went on to buy the three freight companies and Railfreight Distribution, with dire consequences for the Class 47 fleet.

More modifications

Further modification to the fleet commenced in April 1983 with the fitment of a speed sensor to make the locos suitable for Driver Only Operation. The equipment would instigate a brake application if the direction controller was put into 'engine only' while the loco was moving and was situated behind the number 2 end headcode panel, altered during the work. Freight locos were generally fitted before the passenger ones.

A further change in June 1983 was the fitment of high intensity headlights to make trains more visible to track workers. It took the best part of five years to fit the entire fleet, with 47008 the last in February 1988. The installation of National Radio Network (NRN) aerials on cab roofs took place from autumn 1987 onwards, with the last ones added in 1990.

The idea of fitting auxiliary fuel tanks to some Class 47s was first mooted in 1980, but it was not until the release of 47650 in July 1986 that the concept came to fruition (barring the 47/7s). The original fuel tanks held 720 gallons, giving a range of 500 miles with a heavy load. The fitment of an underslung 500-gallon tank meant that the journeys from Kings Cross to Aberdeen and Newcastle to Penzance could be undertaken by a single loco.

Many of the Petroleum sector locos were also internally modified with

A pair of Class 47s (47246 and 47474) are joined by Class 50 50017 at the Ranelagh Bridge fuel point outside Paddington on July 22, 1978. The clean roof of ex-works 47246 clearly shows the plated over boiler exhaust port and also the two-piece moveable radiator louvres at the No 1 end.
(Gavin Morrison)

It seems scarcely believable, but 47216 was renumbered 47299 in December 1981 after a clairvoyant predicted the loco would be involved in a fatal collision

www.railwaysillustrated.co.uk

SULZER POWER 95

FEATURE | Brush Type 4 (Class 47)

Network SouthEast-liveried 47583 leads Large Logo 47438 in Sonning Cutting with the 1000 Oxford to Paddington on August 29, 1991.
(John Whiteley)

At the time on hire to GB Railfreight, Class 47/8s 47812 and 47843 pass Whitley Bridge Junction with the 4D19 1228 Drax to Doncaster gypsum working on August 12, 2014.
(John Whiteley)

additional fuel tanks in the former boiler compartment.

At Tinsley in March 1994, 47150/152 were fitted with Green Circle Multiple working and renumbered 47399/398 for use by the Railfreight Distribution (RfD) sector. Further conversions and re-numberings followed and the programme was so successful that the number sequence was exhausted and the locos reverted to their former numbers in 1995.

Later, under privatisation, Colas also went on to install the Green Circle system in its 47s, whereas DRS used the Blue Star system on its four examples.

The opening of the Willesden Royal Mail hub saw the need for trains to reverse to access the terminal. To avoid using a drawback loco communication, a propelling control vehicle PCV was set up via RCH cables, which Res fitted to its refurbished locos renumbered in the 47/7 series, as well as 47566/624/628/635/640. The equipment was tested between Derby and Leicester using 47704 in May 1996 and further on the West Somerset initially using 47733 in August.

Class 97

Four Departmental 47s, 47472/480/545/561, were renumbered as Class 97s in September 1988 for use on RTC test trains, although they still saw frequent use on passenger trains. However, there were problems when some drivers refused to take them as they "did not sign 97s" and they were renumbered back to 47s in the 4797x series from July 1989. The RTC eventually got its own fleet of six 47s, which were permitted to run at 100mph on test trains, while 47971/4-6 were also fitted with a form of Blue Star multiple working during 1990, allowing them to propel RTC driving vehicles.

Class 57

In October 1997, 47356 arrived at Loughborough to be converted to 57001 after Freightliner signed a £3m contract with Brush to fit six Class 47s with second-hand GM power units and Class 56 alternators. The Sulzer power unit was deemed responsible for 38 per cent of Freightliner failures and the changes would also allow a 57 to haul 1,600 tons on the Felixstowe branch, compared to 960 tons for a standard Class 47, meaning the company would no longer need to hire in Class 56s. In total 33 Class 47s were converted to Class 57.

The end of loco haulage

CrossCountry ceased using 47s on a daily basis in 2002, although they returned to use on Midland Main Line and on the Holyhead-Birmingham route for Arriva

At the time part of the Direct Rail Services fleet, 47790, wearing Northern Belle colours, passes Colton South Junction with a Rugby to York Northern Belle railtour on October 22, 2011. (John Whiteley)

The standard Class 47 driving cab (47767), as refurbished by Crewe Works for use with Rail express systems (RES): **1** automatic brake valve (train air or vacuum brakes and proportionally the air brakes on the loco), **2** AWS sunflower indicator, **3** straight air brake valve (loco only), **4** headlight switch, **5** main reservoir air pressure gauge, **6** bogie brake cylinder pressure gauge, **7** vacuum gauge, **8** speedometer, **9** brake pipe pressure gauge, **10** traction motor overload reset button, **11** main generator/alternator output, **12** electric train supply on and off buttons, **13** fire alarm test button, **14** brake overcharge button, **15** cab heat switch, **16** driver's ash-tray, **17** driver's safety device pedal, **18** AWS reset button, **19** light display (left to right engine stop light [red], wheelslip light [amber], alarm light [blue]), **20** warning horn valve, **21** master key socket, **22** engine start/stop buttons, **23** main power controller (with anti-slip button in red knob), **24** master switch, **25** electric train heat supply warning light dimmer switch, **26** cab shore telephone, **27** electric train heat (supply) warning light, **28** switches [left to right] tail light switch, demister switch, desk light switch, marker light switch, **29** switches [left to right] compartment light switch, foot rest warmer, cab heat driver's side, cab heat secondman's side. (Colin Marsden)

FEATURE | Brush Type 4 (Class 47)

Wearing the hard to miss red scheme of Rail Express Systems, 47492 near Penmaenmawr with the 0840 Euston to Holyhead service on July 19, 1997. (John Whiteley)

Almost BR blue, but not quite. Advenza Railfreight's 47237 stabled at York in June 2008. The loco is now part of the West Coast Railways fleet. (Rail Photoprints/Colin Whitfield)

Class 47/0 47276 makes a typical smoky sight as it restarts a short freight at Wrawby Junction heading towards Immingham on August 29, 1992. (John Whiteley)

Trains Wales. Great Western continued to use 47s until 2004 when they were usurped by Class 57s; indeed April 1, 2004 marked the first time since 1963 that the type had no booked passenger work.

Export

Talks took place between Ferrocarriles Nacionales de Cuba (Cuban National Railways) and British Railways regarding the possible purchase of diesel locos. The following year an order for ten based around the Brush/Sulzer Type 4 was placed, numbered 2501-10. In the years immediately after the Cuban Missile Crisis, the project was politically sensitive: Brush's parent company Hawker-Siddeley was heavily involved in the defence industry and this new deal could be frowned upon by the USA. A huge cover up was organised and led to the locos being built by the Clayton Equipment Company in Hatton, Derby and delivered with Clayton builders plates. However, the bodyshells and some internal equipment were assembled at the Brush Works in Loughborough.

Testing of the finished locos was performed at night between Derby and Burton upon Trent, but due to them being fitted with incompatible Cuba couplers, the locos only ran light engine. Another recognisable difference to their UK counterparts was the large cab roof-mounted headlight, while the locos also had larger cooling equipment to deal with the warmer Cuban climate. They were powered by a French-built Sulzer 2,534hp 12LVA24, rated at 1,050rpm – the same unit as fitted to the Class 48s. There was no train heating equipment, but air brakes were standard. A colour scheme similar to BR's two-tone green was applied, but much later they were painted red with white banding and a chevron around the can side.

To accommodate them, work on UK locos D1842-61 was transferred to Crewe. The ten were exported via Hull Docks between July 30 and November 21, 1965. It is believed all ten were withdrawn by 1992 and have since been scrapped.

In October 2015, 47375 left the Nemesis facility at Burton on a low loader bound for Rotterdam. Paperwork issues saw it stranded at the Dutch port for several months before it finally moved to its intended destination, Hungary. On May 27, 2017 it became the first 47 to work a passenger train away from the UK mainland when it worked a tour out of Budapest.

Privateers

Fragonset entered the spot-hire market in 1997 with locos bought from the disillusioned Pete Waterman, with 47701 and 47703 its first locos to be main line certified that July. After a steady start Fragonset went on to acquire more, many of them derelict, at an alarming rate. It went on to merge with Merlin to become FM Rail, but the expansion was too fast and the company collapsed. West Coast Railway Company, on the other hand, was granted its operating licence on June 1, 1998, but it was May 2003 before it bought its first main line loco – 47854. WCR is still with us today, but many other companies such as Cotswold and Riviera have come and gone as operators of Class 47s. The history of the Class 47s continues to be written though, following the purchase of three 47s from Colas by GB Railfreight in December 2017. S